Praise for **Deep Thought Strategy**

"*Steve Lowell shares the most powerful positioning concept we ALL need to apply: "uncover the problem your prospects don't yet know they have." BOOM."*

~ Brian Walter, CSP, CPAE
President of Extreme Meetings
Past President of the National Speakers Association

"**Deep Thought Strategy** *is brilliant. Over the past several years I have seen Steve Lowell take individuals from obscurity to Success, Influence, Impact and Wealth. His words of wisdom and guidance are world-renowned, effective and life changing. He truly has changed my business in ways no one else ever has. Do yourself a favour and share with anyone and everyone who wants to achieve success in life and business."*

~ Judy O'Beirn, International Bestselling Author and
President, Hasmark Publishing International

"*Steve Lowell has written a remarkable book, which is a valuable, readable and usable guide to becoming the only person in your niche with whom people wish to work. Steve describes a clear process, provides real-world examples and an the book is written in an easy style.* **Deep Thought Strategy** *should be on the bookshelf of everyone who wants to grow their business and become seen as 'the one'. I cannot recommend it highly enough."*

~ Alan Stevens, Media Coach
Past President, Global Speakers Federation

D1615049

"*Steve Lowell is magic! His book resonates his philosophies of how to be successful while working on branding and messaging from the heart. I have had the privilege of meeting Steve and the wind beneath his wings, Jayne Lowell. Together, they are a powerhouse and a true inspiration.*"

~ Pashmina P., International Bestselling Author,
The Cappuccino Chronicles Trilogy
Marketing Manager, Hasmark Publishing International

"*I first saw Steve's Repumeter concept in 2015 when he presented it for the Canadian Association of Professional Speakers. I was blown away by the clarity that it provided the audience on how to stand out and differentiate themselves. Reading this book will provide you with an incredible asset called "Your Expert Insights" which will position you as the only logical choice in your field.*"

~ Nabil Doss, Expert in Influential Communication
Past President of the Global Speakers Federation
Past President of the Canadian Association of
Professional Speakers

Before you get started...
Steve has a message for you...

ZAP IT

Download the Zappar app
(or visit web.zappar.com)
and then scan this code to find the message.

READY
Download Zappar
for free from
the AppStore or
Google Play

ZAP
Aim at the
zapcode
and scan

LEARN
Watch images,
animations and
videos come to
life on the page!

DEEP THOUGHT
STRATEGY

How to go from OBSCURITY to
**Success, Influence, Impact
and Wealth**

STEVE LOWELL

Hasmark
PUBLISHING
INTERNATIONAL

To my incredible wife, Jayne.

Not a single one of these pages would have ever been written if it weren't for you. You still take my cool away!

ACKNOWLEDGEMENTS

Crafting a body of work of any significance depends highly on the support of one's tribe. I am blessed to have a large tribe of supportive advocates who have collectively made it possible for this body of work to exist. It would be impossible to name every person who has influenced the creation of this book. Of particular note are the following:

My wife, Jayne who made way for the mental and emotional space required for me to have the time and the inspiration to complete the book. She not only supported this effort, but she encouraged it and, on more than a few occasions kicked my butt to get me into action to make it happen.

To Jeanette and Theo, thank you for allowing us the use of your incredible cottage where the bulk of this book was written. Your private paradise was the perfect environment to make this happen.

Thank you to my Mom and dad; Jim and Eileen who encourage and inspire Jayne and me to keep doing what we do. Your unconditional love and support is not only an inspiration to us as a couple, but an example of how life should be lived; with love.

To all of my clients around the globe; I thank you for giving me the opportunity to offer my gifts to you so that you may bring your gifts to this world and create wealth by doing it.

To the dedicated and hard-working team at Hasmark Publishing. You were available to us at any time on a moment's notice. Your persistence, expertise and your dedication to excellence is apparent on every page.

And finally, to all of my teachers over the years including (but not limited to), Anil Agrawal, Mr. Cummings, Rima Aristocrat and Dave Falle; your collective influence has formed the foundation of who I have become.

To each and every one of you, I thank you!

Table of Contents

PART TWO
The Repumeter™

PART THREE
Deep Thought Strategy Prerequisites

FOREWORD

The premise of this book, *"Deep Thought Strategy"* is intriguing because it challenges conventional thought about business and personal development; advice given by many success coaches and motivational speakers who espouse the virtues of thinking big.

In this book Steve challenges this paradigm through his own experience over a lifetime of entrepreneurship, failed business pursuits and finally global success found through thinking deep.

Steve demonstrates how thinking big as a strategy fails for most people, and by thinking deeper before thinking bigger; deploying a deep thought strategy, one can expedite their journey to success without having to endure the inevitable failures that are so often associated with thinking big. All this happens by positioning yourself as the only logical choice within your circles.

Steve will introduce you to The Repumeter™; a tool that measures the state of your reputation. By changing your approach to your business and applying deeper thought, you can begin building your plan to stand out and get noticed. Throughout this book, Steve reveals why this is important and how to implement the knowledge and insights gained so our respective reputations and businesses evolve, grow and prosper, regardless of our industry or our field of expertise. The Repumeter™ prepares you for thinking bigger by first showing you how to think deeper.

Additionally, you'll meet Steve's wife, Jayne, his partner in life as well as in business. You'll learn that Steve credits Jayne's ability to help people with their mindsets and their abilities to move forward positively in their lives and businesses. He knows this, not because Jayne is his wife, but because she helped him change his perspective and his mindset before they fell in love, before they married.

As you work through this book and apply the principles, strategies and techniques to your own business, I urge you to jot down your own ideas as you read. Review them later, apply those that make sense for you and your business and you too will be able to enhance your reputation, grow your business, and finally enjoy the benefits of thinking big.

Susan Luke Evans
CSP, Global Speaking Fellow
Toronto, Ontario, Canada

PREFACE

Thinking Big vs. Thinking Deep

For over 35 years now I have been hearing it. "You have to think BIGGER!" "You need BIG, SCARY GOALS!" "If you're going to think anyway, THINK BIG!" And for 30 of those years I bought into the illusion that thinking big would help me grow my business. I was wrong. The purpose of this book is to guide you through a process that will make thinking big a winning strategy instead of a losing one.

I thought big my whole life. I have been studying personal development for my entire adult life. There's not much out there in the personal development space that I have not studied, practiced and even taught. And all of it includes some form of advice around thinking big, but there was always something missing. It took me 30 years to figure out what it was, and you'll learn all about the missing piece in these pages.

The missing piece is a parcel of wisdom that comes from inside you called your "expert insights," which are found through a process called your deep thought strategy. This book walks you through the deep thought strategy process to help you find your own expert insights. With this preparation, when the time comes for you to think big, you'll be ready and properly equipped.

The problem with thinking big as a strategy is that it sets you up for near certain failure. Thinking big by itself doesn't validate that whatever you're doing now is even possible in a bigger game. Through a deep thought strategy, you'll validate the scalability of

iv	Deep Thought Strategy

your business before you make mission-critical decisions on a bigger scale and know how to position yourself for a much bigger game.

A concept of universal law has been popularized in America and abroad over the last few decades; especially since the movie "The Secret" was released in 2006. In the movie many of the most popular personal development gurus of the time assembled and collectively evangelized "the Law of Attraction" as the secret to manifesting that which you desire through the energetic and vibrational properties of thought and emotion.

Though "The Secret" shined the light on the Law of Attraction in 2006, theories of universal law have been taught since before the Chinese classic text "Tao Te Ching" was written by Lao Tzu sometime between the 4th and 6th century BC.

What the gurus seem to agree on is there are many universal laws that govern our experience, though the number, names and functions of the universal laws vary widely depending on who you talk to. What I have noticed is regardless of what brand of universal law theory they subscribe to, so many people dilute the collective meaning of the universal laws and wrap them up into a single concept; anything is possible so let's think big.

I know people who have set goals for themselves that are simply unattainable without Divine intervention. I know some who have placed unconditional offers on multi-million-dollar homes when they have no assets or income to support such a purchase. Of course, the deals fell through and they were on the hook for tens of thousands of dollars in real estate fees and penalties.

Others have signed a lease on a luxury vehicle knowing their income won't cover the payments, only to have the vehicle repossessed and their credit destroyed.

Some have a few good months in their network marketing business and somehow convince a bank to lend them a million dollars, only to end up going bankrupt when they can't pay back the loan.

These are all real examples of real people who fell into the trap of thinking bigger without first thinking deeper, only to be forced back into playing small as a result. Sometimes the damage is so great that they never recover and end up playing small forever.

Maybe you're not making those kinds of decisions (which is a good thing). Maybe you're a businessperson or sales professional who really wants to play a bigger game, and who has tried playing a bigger game but just seems to be having trouble advancing on a bigger scale.

If that's you, then you're in the right place! You are about to discover how to prepare for thinking big by first thinking deep. You'll read how a deep thought strategy helps unknown speakers become award-winning international speakers. You'll discover how a local consultant in Singapore wins international business and how a former mental health patient gets hired to speak at international conferences – all through their own deep thought strategy.

Yes, there is a time for thinking big, but not before some preparatory work is done first. Thinking big can work. It can take you to levels you never knew were possible. But before you seriously begin thinking bigger, let me urge you to first prepare yourself by thinking deeper.

Deeper precedes bigger every time.

Deeper before bigger is what the deep thought strategy is all about. It has worked for me, and it will work for you too!

Now, let's get started and get you thinking deeper, so you can properly prepare yourself for thinking bigger, doing bigger and winning bigger by positioning yourself as the only logical choice via your deep thought strategy.

PART ONE

How I Arrived at Deep Thought Strategy

WHAT IS
DEEP THOUGHT STRATEGY?

Deep thought strategy is a prerequisite to thinking big. It's a process by which we explore our business expertise and our clients' condition at the forensic level in search of what I call our "expert insights."

"Expert insights" is a term I use to describe a perspective that comes from deep within your experience and of which only you can claim ownership. Your expert insights allow you to position yourself as being unique in your field by presenting to your prospects and audiences a snapshot of their world that they have never considered before, and then positioning yourself strategically and tactically as the only logic solution or "THE One."

By first bringing your prospects' or audiences' awareness to a problem they never knew they had and then positioning yourself as "The One," you not only make yourself indispensable, but you eliminate competition and clear the path for thinking bigger. That's a deep thought strategy.

LESSONS FROM A VACUUM SALESMAN

It was early 1980s, I sold vacuum cleaners; Filter Queen.

We had a great system for generating leads; when I went to a home to demonstrate the Filter Queen, the prospect already knew I was there to do a vacuum cleaner demonstration. The only reason they would agree to see the demonstration is because we enticed them with gifts just for watching the demonstration.

Our sales presentation was brilliant. I had no idea how it would become relevant to me in my 50s.

Almost every sales call goes pretty much the same way. As they invite me into their home, my prospect would tell me how there is no chance of me making a sale today. Thirty minutes later we're at the kitchen table negotiating a payment plan on a $2,500 vacuum. If there was no sale to be made, it was almost always about the prospect's ability to pay, never a question of the prospect wanting the machine.

Our basic sales approach was this:

1. Put the prospect at ease. Chat a little to warm up the room, "Here's your free gift, I understand you won't be buying anything today, this will only take a few minutes."

2. Spend a minute or two pulling the machine out of the box and talk about it a little.

3. Attach the hose to the machine along with the "dust scope;" a small device with a white filter that captures whatever the vacuum picks up.

4. Turn the vacuum on, push the nozzle over about six inches of floor and stop.

5. Open up the dust scope and show the prospect the pile of dust, sand and dirt they never even knew was there; pause and let them imagine how dirty their entire home must be.

6. Walk them to the kitchen table and start filling out the sales contract.

Of course, not every call was quite that simple, but many of them were, and most were not much more complicated.

At the time I was simply following a predetermined sales process. I had no idea that I was applying principles that would become so powerful in my business as a speaker.

Here's what I now know from that experience; no prospect was interested in the Filter Queen until they became aware of a problem they never knew they had. Once they became aware of the problem; massive amounts of dirt and germs right where their children play, all they cared about was solving that problem.

Why is this relevant to you? Because although the scale is different, the principle is very similar. Your deep thought strategy prepares you to uncover the problem your prospects and audiences don't yet know they have, and then positions you as the only logical choice.

DEEP THOUGHT STRATEGY AT WORK

I do this all the time.

I walk out onto the stage, look at my audience and ask this question, "Put up your hand if you or someone you know is in the market for a tennis instructor."

I have done this with audiences of a few and audiences of hundreds and the results are always the same. With the very odd exception when maybe one or two hands might go up, no one ever puts their hand up for this question. People simply aren't in the market for a tennis instructor.

But then I challenge them a little, "If you look around the room, you'll see that no one is in the market for a tennis instructor. But I'm going to estimate that at least 25 of you (or 50 or more depending on the size of the audience… I usually go for about 25% of the audience at least) are either in the market for a tennis instructor yourself right now, or you know someone who is."

Then I tell them about Brian.

After I tell them about Brian, I ask them again, "Put up your hand if you know someone who's in the market for a tennis instructor."

The results are always the same. I never miss. The hands fly into the air and I begin to count them off one by one until I reach my estimate; and there are always more hands in the air than what I estimated.

Now, to understand what just happened, you'll need to meet Brian.

Brian was doing all the right things to grow his business:

• He went to networking events

• He met the right kind of people

• He told them who he was and what he did

He had this networking thing down to a science. In fact, whenever there was a networking opportunity, whether at a specified event or just talking over coffee or sharing thoughts while at the gym, Brian was there. He was always promoting his business. He was exchanging business cards, making follow up calls, and then going to yet another event.

And yet, his business wasn't growing, people weren't paying attention to what he was offering, or maybe they just didn't care. Regardless of the reasons people had, and regardless of how many hours Brian spent networking or distributing flyers, taking out ads on social media or offering special promotional deals, the bottom line was the same – Brian was not making the progress he needed to be both successful and profitable.

Brian did what most of us would do. He started thinking bigger, and this was his biggest mistake.

You see, when we start thinking bigger it typically translates to doing more. More of the same. More hours. More effort. More expense. And we do it all under the guise of thinking bigger, when all we're really doing is thinking and working ourselves into exhaustion. And when the results don't follow, we begin to doubt that bigger is possible for us and so we revert back to thinking and playing small.

Thinking bigger by itself is not a strategy for growth, it's a strategy for almost certain failure. Why? Because for most of us thinking bigger can only result in DOING bigger unless it's preceded by something that prepares us for doing bigger, and that something is what I call "thinking deeper."

If we don't think deeper in addition to thinking bigger, our path to success is a troubled one. That's what was happening to Brian.

Brian came to me with his dilemma and I asked, "What do you do?"

"I'm a tennis instructor," he answered.

Well, based on what happens with every single audience I have spoken to all over the world you can clearly see what the market is for a tennis instructor.

But Brian was convinced that if he just thought bigger and did more, the results would come, but they never did and so he came to me.

I taught Brian three fundamental principles about positioning and networking. These three principles form the foundation upon which the rest of this book is based. It all starts with you understanding these three simple things:

1. Many marketing people say you need to be different from your competitors. In reality you don't need to be different from everyone else who does what you do, you only need to *appear* to be different.

2. You appear to be different by changing the language you use about yourself.

3. Your message must be easy to understand and easily repeated (unlike elevator pitches).

Brian realized that what he actually did (as a tennis instructor) was to take kids (technically of any age) and basically 'wear them out' on the tennis court. At the end of each session, he turned them over to their parents, physically exhausted, happy with learning or enhancing their skills, and perhaps, from time to time, a feeling of success because of their accomplishments.

Now when people ask Brian what he does, he replies, "You know how sometimes kids have so much energy that they're bouncing off the walls, and their parents get frustrated because they don't know what to do with them? I take kids of any age to a tennis court, I absolutely exhaust them, and then I hand them back to their parents."

Naturally, almost everyone in every audience experiences an unruly child from time to time or, at the very least knows someone who does.

So, when I ask the audience for the second time to put up their hand if they know someone who is in the market for a tennis instructor, everyone who has any experience with children anywhere in their lives puts up their hand.

Since Brian, the tennis instructor first came to me, he has become known as 'the guy who tires your kids out on a tennis court.' Suddenly lots of parents and grandparents have a "need" for a tennis instructor – a need they didn't know they had, until Brian gave them a little snapshot of their world they hadn't considered before, "what if I could totally exhaust your child or grandchild and do it safely?"

There are four points to this story.

The first point: Brian was leaving a ton of business on the table every single time he made himself look and sound like every other tennis instructor by using the same language, "I'm a tennis instructor."

The second point: Simply by changing his language he was able to stand out and get noticed, even if he wasn't really all that different from other tennis instructors.

The third point: By changing his language a certain way, his message became memorable and repeatable by anyone who ever sees kids bouncing off the walls. Where's that tennis guy who exhausts kids?

The fourth point: Brian didn't expand his business by thinking bigger. He expanded his business by thinking deeper. Once he learned to do that, thinking bigger happened all by itself. That's where we're going with all of this.

Nice story, huh? Yet you're probably saying to yourself, "That's great for a tennis instructor, but how do I adapt that same kind of change to how I promote my business or product?"

It's a good question, and that's exactly what this book is about. It's about you not looking the same as everyone else who does what you do. It's about you not getting caught up in the "think big" myth. It's about you not being a "tennis instructor."

Sometimes it only takes a slight change, such as Brian made, but often it's a longer process.

Usually it takes more time, effort and insight into your own business, the language you are using, and figuring out what to change. That's what I call "thinking deeper."

The purpose of thinking deeper is to discover what to change in your approach that will cause "bigger" to happen without you trying to force it.

The first step? Becoming aware that thinking bigger is not the answer to doing bigger. At least, not all by itself. You need to learn to think deeper first.

Let me share with you how I came to that conclusion. It took me a lifetime of failures to learn it, but all you need to do is read on.

The Origins of Deep Thought Strategy

Somewhere in mid 2007 it struck me. My big chance. My big idea. The answer to all my prayers.

I found myself embedded into a virtual network marketing group called "Vision 100K." It was being built as a training ground for network marketers to learn advanced skills without having to leave their current business.

The founders were a couple of Canadian guys who had both been very successful in network marketing (sometimes called "multi-level marketing" or "MLM"). One of these guys was living in Costa Rica and ran the whole venture virtually from there.

It was the first time I had witnessed online conferencing and we held all of our meetings through an online conferencing system.

The guy in Costa Rica was Bob. He was the visionary and hosted all of the virtual meetings.

One day I was listening to the radio at home in Ottawa, and there was an announcement for an upcoming event called "The Sales Executive Roundtable." It was a mastermind-type event that sales executives would pay to attend and share ideas with each other. From that announcement, my big idea was born: "The MLM Executive Roundtable."

I would host regular live, virtual events where network marketers from around the globe would gather and share business strategies and best practices. In addition, I would provide speaking, presenting and sales training.

Members would pay $100 per month; we would have a thousand members, schedule virtual meetings to accommodate the various time zones and invite network marketers of all kinds to join us. It was brilliant!

I got to work at once!

By the next morning I was in business. I had the website, the registration page, the sales copy, the payment system and the event schedule completed. I was ready to take registrations. I was so excited! I could see a thousand people in the system, all receiving high-value content and training and I would be bringing in $100,000 per month in no time. I was thinking big, and this time it was fool proof!

I called Bob, the guy in Costa Rica. My story was flying out of my mouth at about 600 words per minute. My voice was sharp, my excitement was over the top as I reeled off my vision to Bob.

"Bob, I have it! It's the best idea of the century! It's called the MLM Executive Roundtable. I'm going to get a thousand people to pay $100 each per month. We'll hold regular virtual meetings to help them all become better network marketers. They'll each bring in their entire downline and it will be the biggest MLM organization in the world! What do you think, Bob? Isn't this the greatest idea ever??"

Bob responded with two words.

Two words that will suck the life force out of any dream, "Yeah but…"

"Yeah but, how are you going to find the people and get them to register for this thing?" Bob asked.

But I was ready for him! I knew Bob was going to ask me that question and I had my answer already planned. I had already given this a ton of thought and I had a strategy. I was thinking big and I knew if I was going to think big, I needed to take big action and so I had it all planned out.

"Bob, I have already thought of that! I'm going to use… the Law of Attraction! I'm going to vibrate, Bob! You know as well as I do that when you vibrate at the right frequency, the universe conspires to assemble all the resources you need to make any dream a reality!"

At least, that's what they said in the movie "The Secret" when it came out in November 2006. In fact, I'd learned about the Law of Attraction when I attended a private retreat with one of the stars of the movie two years before the movie premiered.

I was truly convinced. I was thinking big, I had a plan, I took action and I vibrated. It's pretty easy to surmise how many registrations I got. Zero.

Yes, I fell deeply into the "thinking big" illusion, got caught up in the whole Law of Attraction hype and I made decisions and took actions based on lore and not legitimate business rationale. I didn't think deep enough.

This is what happens when we use thinking big as the foundation of a strategy, nothing except wasted effort, time, energy and expense.

I have learned so much since then. That's not to say that I never made the same mistakes again, I did. Many times, some of which you will read about in these pages.

I believed and still believe in the Law of Attraction. I do believe in thinking big and I do believe with all my soul that our mindset and belief systems have a critical role to play in our success and that the universe can and does deliver everything we need to succeed. I have experienced irrefutable evidence since 2007. I just needed to find the right formula to apply all these elements so that they could be positioned to operate according to their natural processes. I hadn't found that formula yet. But I wasn't about to give up!

Life went on. I worked very hard in my business and I was making some headway building my business slowly the old-fashioned way, through hard work, focus and constant learning. One small step at a time. I'm not suggesting that's the way it always has to be; I'm simply saying that's what happened with me.

This was certainly not the first time I got caught in the thinking big illusion, nor would it be the last. I had been doing it all my life and I would continue to do it for a number of years afterwards.

WHAT IF I HAD APPLIED A DEEP THOUGHT STRATEGY

When I launched the MLM Executive Roundtable, I was thinking big in that I was attempting to get lots of people paying into something that would make lots of money.

Bob (the one who lived in Costa Rica) asked me how I was going to find those people. He asked me the wrong question. The right question would have been "Why would those people join?"

The concept of the MLM Executive Roundtable was a good concept. The bigness of the thought behind it was also appropriate. The problem was that I used the big idea itself as a strategy. The deep thought strategy to properly set up the whole thing was missing. What would position the MLM Executive Roundtable to be the only logical choice, THE One, not in my mind, but in the minds of my audience?

If I had presented something to my audience which brought their awareness to a problem they never knew they had, revealed to them something about their world that they had never considered before; they would have had a reason to at least explore it. A deep thought strategy would have revealed these things and prepared me to take strategic and tactical action. I didn't do that, so the project failed.

YOUR STAGE:
MORE THINKING BIGGER

Sometime in 2009 my good buddy, Bob (not the MLM guy who lived in Costa Rica, another Bob from Ottawa) and I were chatting after a networking breakfast that Bob had hosted. During the conversation I mentioned to Bob an idea I had. We would hold a meeting once per month on a Friday morning where people could come and not only network but learn as well.

I would do speaking training with live, on-stage coaching and Bob would do personal development training with meditations and other exercises. We would give local entrepreneurs an opportunity to be guest speakers and we would provide an excellent breakfast for as low a fee as we could arrange.

At our first session we had 18 people attend. Within pretty short order we were getting 70 to 80 people attending. Even though it was costing me money every month to run the event, Bob and I both loved the experience. For Bob it was about the people and the social equity. For me it was also an opportunity to try new material, get some video footage and get my name known in the area.

Attendance seemed to stall at about 80 attendees and then, after the first couple of years it began to decline.

I could tell that it was well known in the area because I would hear people talk about it when they didn't know I was listening. I heard nothing but really good things about Your Stage and my Facebook following was growing fast. I was making a name for myself because of Your Stage and I was feeling pretty good about it.

I could see the event was beginning to stagnate, so I thought we needed an injection of interest from a new audience. I started thinking bigger! I wanted to find a way to bring more people to Your Stage with more horsepower than inviting them one at a time.

I found out that a local Chamber of Commerce was meeting at the same venue and on the same day as Your Stage for a single session. Not only was it at the same venue on the same day, but their meeting was in the very next room to ours. It was a special meeting of the Chamber, so they were expecting a couple of hundred people in attendance. The Chamber of Commerce meeting ran from 7:00 AM to 8:30 AM. Your Stage always started at 9:00 AM with doors opening at 8:30 AM. That gave me an idea!

I contacted the organizer of the Chamber of Commerce meeting and I invited the entire Chamber of Commerce to attend Your Stage immediately after their meeting as my personal guests. They loved the idea! In fact, not only did they announce the invitation to their entire database two weeks before their meeting, they even invited me to join their meeting and provide a two-minute live invitation right before they closed.

I was so excited!

I announced to our entire Your Stage database that the next meeting would be super-sized. We had invited the entire Chamber of Commerce audience to join us and this would make for an amazing opportunity for networking, connecting and learning. It would be epic!

As the day approached, I could envision the room filled with 200 or more people, maybe 300 or more!

I arranged to have the venue set up the room for 200 people but had them stand by to add chairs when the room filled up.

I rented bigger sound equipment to handle the much larger crowd. I ordered extra coffee for everyone, planned my content for the morning and found the strongest speakers I could find.

A few days before it was all to happen, Bob informed me that he could not attend. Something had come up and, as much as he wanted to be there, it just wasn't possible. He felt horrible, but it just couldn't be helped.

No matter, I knew how to do everything, so I had it all planned out. We had a regular volunteer who worked the registration desk at Your Stage, and she would be there to handle the regular Your Stage crowd. I would find a volunteer to generally manage the mingling at Your Stage while I ducked out to the Chamber of Commerce meeting next door, made an appearance and extended the personal invitation to join us next door.

At 8:00 AM my volunteers were in place, the room for Your Stage was set up, I had set up the sound gear, breakfast was ready for my Your Stagers, the extra coffee was ready to be served and everything was set!

At Your Stage people generally started arriving at about 8:10, the room was usually filled by 8:30. They would mingle, network and enjoy a buffet breakfast until 9:00 when the formal program begins. This would give the Chamber of Commerce folks time to exit their meeting, use the rest rooms and join us at Your Stage during the networking and maybe grab an additional plate of breakfast if they liked.

It was perfect!

As I was sitting in my chair at the Chamber of Commerce meeting, I could hardly contain my excitement. I knew that we would have a record crowd at Your Stage because of the excitement of having the entire Chamber of Commerce join us, and I knew that room beside me would fill up fast!

I made my announcement to the entire Chamber of Commerce audience, invited them to join us as my personal guests to experience the mighty Your Stage! I would be there at the door to welcome them as soon as their meeting adjourned.

In a few minutes, as the Chamber meeting came to a close, I headed out the door and made my way over to Your Stage.

As I walked into the room, I thought I was going to die! It was a record-breaking crowd! Never in the history of the event had we ever seen, or even imagined an audience of this size.

Eight people!

That was it! A measly eight people showed up for Your Stage.

As my guests from next door stepped up one by one, they peered into the huge empty room, turned around and left.

I was devastated and humiliated. But I was also a professional. I was obliged to provide an outstanding experience to each and every one of those people who did show up, and I did. I gave everything I had left to make that meeting the best it could possibly be. Those who did stay told me how much value they received because of the intimate experience and the focused discussions that occurred.

On that day I decided to close Your Stage for good. It was only after I vented to a friend of mine who convinced me to keep going that I reconsidered and decided to try again. I'm not sure where that fortitude came from, it was just there.

Bob and I continued to offer Your Stage for the next several months without much effort or initiative. We loved doing it. It became a hobby. But that didn't last long for me. I needed more. I needed forward motion. I needed something bigger.

Bob and I decided to try again to take Your Stage to a whole new level. Once again, we decided to think bigger.

We brought in a new partner, a business mentor of mine named Anil. You'll read more of Anil in "Part Three: Deep Thought Strategy Prerequisites."

We created a whole new strategy for Your Stage that up-leveled the experience. This included creating a new and more robust membership plan and developing a brand-new website with all the membership features we needed. We also increased our promotion efforts, made more phone calls, promoted more on social media, looked for sponsors, went to more networking events to promote Your Stage. We kept thinking bigger, doing more, investing more trying to become more; and we did this for months.

As months became years, we were getting really frustrated because we were working hard, trying everything we could think of and nothing was working. We couldn't make a decent living with this at all.

Like a lot of other small business owners, we had to do other things, because we weren't making a living with Your Stage.

For us, thinking bigger meant doing more. We did more; we failed… again and again.

Eventually, Anil had to leave for personal reasons. Bob and I came to the conclusion that as long as our expenses were covered and if there was a little beer money left over after the meetings, we would be happy with that.

So, we reverted back to playing small. Sure, we had loads of fun. But for a business venture, it simply wasn't happening and we both lost the belief that it could. Once the belief evaporated, so eventually did the enthusiasm.

I began to seriously question what I should do. Should I try again to turn Your Stage into something bigger and better, or should I close it down and try something else?

WHAT IF I HAD APPLIED A DEEP THOUGHT STRATEGY

If I had applied a deep thought strategy when I invited the Chamber of Commerce to join Your Stage, I would have explored some critical questions before I extended the invitation to the Chamber of Commerce:

- Why would Your Stage attendees want the Chamber of Commerce to join them, and vice versa?
- What would that experience provide each group that they needed and couldn't get anywhere else?
- What problem was being solved for both audiences?
- How was bigger actually going to be better for anyone other than me?

I operated under the assumption that bigger would be better for everyone. I also believed that both groups wanted a bigger experience.

A deep thought strategy would have involved reaching three outcomes with each audience before extending the invitation to merge for that one meeting:

1. I would have brought to each audience's awareness a problem they never knew they had. They would have felt missing this meeting left their problem unresolved.

2. Each group would have felt there was a measurable cost associated with missing the event.

3. Your Stagers would have needed to know that the Chamber of Commerce attendees were bringing with them something Your Stagers didn't have and couldn't get anywhere else, and vice versa. Perhaps some specific connection equity, specific opportunities or something else that would enrich their businesses or their lives.

By thinking bigger while not applying a deep thought strategy, all I did was offer more of the same to both groups and try to make it sound exciting, all because I was excited about having a bigger event.

How Thinking Big Kept Me (and My Business) Small

Then something really interesting happened. Someone came to me and said, "Steve, I'm having this event, and I'd like you to train me to speak at the event."

I helped her, and at the event I discovered that most of the speakers on the stage were people I knew. Several of them I had trained at Your Stage. Being curious, I asked the woman who hired me, "Why didn't you ask me to speak at your event?"

She replied with a very intriguing comment, "I didn't know you were an actual speaker."

I said, "Wow!" This was the first time I realized the rest of the world might not think about me the way I thought they did. All the effort we were putting into Your Stage had branded me a certain way. I didn't know this.

I was trying to promote myself as a speaker first, as a speaker-coach second, and this was the first indication that the world was looking at me in a different way. I started to pay more attention and I started attending other people's events. They would have hundreds of people at their events and speakers on the stage whom I had coached, and I wondered again, why hadn't they asked me to speak?

I asked several other people, "I'm curious, why didn't you ask me to speak at your event?" The same answer came up, "I didn't know you were a speaker." I truly didn't understand, how could they not put two and two together?

There was another event being run in Ottawa around this same time. The event planner was a client of mine. I had coached her to speak for this event as well as for several other events. I asked her the same question, "Why haven't you asked me to speak at your event?"

She said something a little bit different. She told me, "I charge my speakers five hundred dollars to get on my stage in front of my audience, and I didn't think *you* could afford it."

I thought, "Huh." The truth is, at that point in time, she was probably right. The perception seemed to be that I was not a speaker and I was not successful. That was another eye-opener for me. I thought, this is very strange.

I went online and actually saw what other people were saying about me in their social media posts. For the first time I started paying attention to what people were saying about me online. If they were saying anything at all, they were talking about Your Stage, the event. Those who attended the event would post about Your Stage. I was not mentioned anywhere other than perhaps a kind, "Thanks, Steve."

When people did talk about me, they said all the wrong things. They said things that branded me as a speaker-coach and not a very successful one. They said things like, "I was at Steve's little speaker training program" and refer to "the three people" at the training. They planted these seeds, making me appear to be very small. The result was my reputation was not growing in a way that was serving me at all.

I noticed an event planner's reputation began to grow and by extension her business began to grow too. I was curious about how she did it. I asked her, "Why have you never been to my Your Stage event?"

She told me if she went to my event, Your Stage, she would be associated with my small brand. She said, "I can't afford to be associated with a small, local meet-up event."

My head reeled, and I thought to myself, "Okay, I thought I was doing myself a favor by creating this event, but she's right! The people in the marketplace perceive me as a speaker-coach who is not very successful and who runs very small events. This is why I go to other people's events where there are 300 people, and I go to mine and there are as few as eight." The reality was my brand was being propagated this way. Thinking big has kept me playing small for years!

Deciding to Become THE One

About a month later, I was going to the venue where we held the Your Stage event. As I walked into the event space, I was astounded by the beautiful Christmas decorations that were everywhere; it was absolutely spectacular, breath-taking, jaw-dropping!!

I asked the woman who ran the venue, "Did you do all this work yourself?"

"No," she said and gave me the name of the decorator. Her next words would change my life: "She's the VERY BEST, she's really EXPENSIVE, IF you can even GET HER."

In my mind I said, "THAT's what I want to be. I want to be known as the VERY BEST! I want to be known as REALLY EXPENSIVE! I want to be known as almost unattainable – IF you can even GET HIM!" Those words inspired me to do it again, to think bigger. So, I did, for a minute or two.

Then reality came crashing back down upon me. Who was I to think I could ever be known as "the very best?"

Sure, to my inner circles I was known as the best at what I did, but I wasn't known anywhere outside my own little circles and my own little events in my own little world.

How would I ever be positioned as "really expensive?"

I was having a hard time giving my services away. I charged next to nothing (and many times nothing) just so I could get some recognition and maybe a referral or two for a little bit of business.

Everyone in my circles knew that I was always around. In fact, not only was I NOT inaccessible, I was everywhere! People often commented on how I was everywhere, and I thought that was a good thing. I could always be found at any event where there was a possibility of getting noticed. I was everywhere because I was thinking bigger, or so I thought!

I wanted the reputation of "he's the very best, he's really expensive, if you can even get him." But instead, thinking bigger had gotten me the reputation of "I hear he's pretty good, he's super cheap and you can find him anywhere."

So, guess what I did.

Yup! I started thinking even bigger! I decided to take on Los Angeles! More on that later, but I'm thinking you can guess how that worked out.

The way forward was pretty obvious to me. I needed to change the way others were speaking about me. I had to somehow take control of what was happening out there in the marketplace.

It was not a quick fix. It took several years to get things changed, and I continued to struggle. I knew my clients were getting good results. I began to take a different kind of action. I set thinking bigger aside and started focusing on getting better rather than bigger.

I committed myself to elevating my own game, as both a speaker and a speaker-coach. I wanted my clients to get more than good results; I wanted my clients to get spectacular results. That's what I focused on.

I'm a voracious reader. I study, I read and I'm dedicated to always honing my craft, to getting better, to improving. I elevated my level of dedication to my craft where my clients were concerned, and I started to see them getting really great results.

Among the first things I did was re-evaluate the veracity of my reach; how many people were actually in my "circle of influence?"

When I explored it, I could clearly see I was connected with lots of people. I attended so many groups and meetings and I had lots of "friends" on Facebook.

But since my high number of connections was not driving much business, I decided to redefine the term "circle of influence" for my own use. I came up with this definition: "The population within which I can catalyze action as it relates to my business."

By this definition it was clear of all the people to whom I was connected, very few were actually influenced by me in a way that related to my business. So, I divided my entire reach into two groups:

- **Circle of influence** – The population within which I can catalyze action as it relates to my business.

- **Circle of connection** – Everyone else I was connected to in any way.

My immediate mandate was to migrate as many people as possible from my circle of connection to my circle of influence.

NOTE: From here on throughout this book, I will refer to the collective as "circles." This term will refer to the total of both groups.

I started collecting testimonials, making sure they were results-based testimonials – not about how nice the event was and not about how nice I was.

Whenever someone would tell me about making sales from the stage, increasing their speaking fee or getting a standing ovation, I would get them on video.

Gradually, people started talking in terms of the results they were getting when they worked with me. I both wanted and needed more. I wanted to get all the people coming to the Your Stage event talking about me; I wanted to turn them into raving fans. And that's what I did. I asked them for testimonials; I helped write the testimonial if necessary. I videotaped them saying it. I soon had a library of powerful, results-oriented testimonials.

My name started floating to the top and referrals started increasing. I started controlling what other people were saying about me and I started to see the conversation shift.

At this point I thought, "I have this group of people from Your Stage, I'm calling my circle of influence, and now they're saying all the right things." The problem was it was all the same people! I had done a great job of teaching them to say the right things about me. However, I needed to increase my circle of influence.

I was overwhelming myself going to Business Network International (BNI) events, the Chamber of Commerce and other networking groups. I was out every single night and every single morning connecting with people – there had to be a better way.

Increasing My
Circle of Influence

During this time, I met Peggy.

Peggy is a popular author and, though I had never met her, I decided to attend a book-launch event she was having just outside Ottawa.

I arrived at the event where roughly 1,000 people had gathered to celebrate Peggy's new book. I was walking along and found myself face to face with Peggy.

I looked at Peggy and said, "So, all this is about you, huh?"

"Yes, it is," she replied. "And who are you?"

Right then I had one of those moments that seemed like a good idea at the time. And what came out of my mouth was, "You don't know me, but you will." And with that, I walked away.

I knew it was a dumb thing to say, but that's what came out.

A while later, I ran into her again. I complemented her on a successful event, and she asked me my name.

Since I had already set the theme in the previous conversation, I felt it would be best to make it look deliberate, so I repeated my statement, "You don't know me, but you will!"

I was thinking she's either intrigued or spooked; either way, she knows I exist. I wasn't sure if that was a good thing or a bad thing. It was what it was.

Close to the end of the event I stepped up to her table where she was signing her books. I purchased a book and handed her the book to sign. She asked me to whom the book should be signed. I looked at her and I repeated, "You don't know me…"

"But I have a feeling that I will," she interrupted.

I gave her my first name and she signed the book.

A few weeks later, I found out that Peggy was speaking at a local event and I wanted to be there.

I was interested to see how she was as a speaker more than anything else.

At the event, before she spoke, Peggy was standing along the wall with another lady whom I did not know. As I walked by, I overheard the lady say to Peggy, "Hey, Steve Lowell is here!"

"Who IS that guy?" Peggy asked.

"He's the speaker guy." The lady replied.

I thought that was interesting. The lady hadn't referred to me as "a speaking coach." She referred to me as "THE speaker guy."

I'm not sure exactly what I read into it at the time, but it certainly was interesting.

After that event, Peggy and I chatted and over some time we became friends. She invited me to come and speak at one of her events in Florida.

At that event, I made a huge impact on Peggy and her audience. I turned Peggy into a fan. I helped her get some great results, and then she referred me to a bunch of people she knew – some of her circle of influence became part of my circle of influence. My association with Peggy began to elevate my profile just a little.

I was beginning to get a reputation of being "the" speaking coach. People started referring me a little more and I was getting some good feedback about the results. I was just beginning to step out of my world of looking small. My business started to grow slowly, but something was still holding me back and I was about to find out what it was.

THOSE CHILDHOOD PATTERNS

In October 2012 I attended an event in Las Vegas. As often happens at big events, I made eye contact with a woman as we passed each other in the hallway. She looked at me with a strange facial expression and said, "I can help you."

I wondered why she thought I needed help; I had not spoken a word. She introduced herself as a psychic. As a point of information, when it came to psychics, I was a cautious (skeptical) believer. I believed in their abilities, but I'd never seen any evidence of it happening. I'm one of those guys who explained everything away in my own head and that was good enough for me. Just because I could explain it away, however, didn't mean it didn't exist.

Nonetheless, I responded politely, and then she said, "There is something in your childhood that is really holding you back. I can't really see what it is, it's not clear, but there's something."

I knew in that moment she was crazy! I had a perfect childhood. Nothing bad ever happened to me in my childhood. She gave me her Facebook details and out of curiosity, a couple weeks later, I reached out and asked for more details about what she'd "seen." She had nothing more to offer; I went on my merry way.

A year or so later I was speaking at an event in Florida. During dinner I was seated at the speakers' table; I didn't know anybody. While all the conversation was going on around me, I noticed a woman sitting directly across from me and she gave me a very familiar look. We didn't have any conversation because everyone was chatting. When there was a break in the conversation, she looked at me and she said, "You know, there's something going on in your childhood…"

My jaw dropped and the "twilight zone" music played in my head. She introduced herself as a psychic and said again, "Yes, there is definitely something going on with you, but I can't really see exactly what it is."

I began to develop a complex.

More time went by and while attending another event, this time in Dallas, a woman seated at the table behind me stood up to ask a question. She introduced herself as a psychic. I was feeling a bit paranoid. But I thought I would try and be open so I decided that I would ask her about my childhood, just in case.

At the break I went to her table to ask her the question. She pointed to me as I approached the table and said, "You want to ask me about your childhood."

It was really weird!

She said, "There's something going on, but I don't know what it is, it's not really clear, but there is definitely something there that's holding you back!"

I wondered if this was some strange conspiracy. What was it, and how was I going to figure it out?

Enter Jayne!

THE JAYNE EFFECT

Weird!! Here I was trying to build my business, thinking bigger all the time and making very little progress, meeting strangers on multiple occasions, and they all said there was something about my childhood that needed to be resolved. I repeat, weird!!

At this point in time, I met Jayne (who was briefly introduced in the Foreword of this book and who is now my wife). Jayne works with mindset, helping people with their belief systems to establish stronger mindsets. And, by the way, she's the VERY BEST, she's REALLY EXPENSIVE, IF you can even GET HER!

Somewhere in our chats I related what had been happening to me, ending with the childhood information these various strangers had mentioned to me and that each of them had said there was "something" in my childhood, but no one knew what.

Jayne said, "I bet I can find it!"

Jayne is not a psychic; however, she is highly intuitive and an amazing listener. She hears things in people's words that draws her attention to a much bigger story. We got together on the phone and she found it.

This is the story: There are three times in our lives while we're growing up that are significant in establishing our belief systems. Generally, something happens between ages two and five, between ages five and 13, and between ages 13 and 20. What happens when we're very young establishes our belief system, what happens in our adolescence confirms our belief system, and what happens in our teenage years validates and locks in our belief system.

The interesting thing is these events don't have to be traumatic to be impactful. That's why I couldn't figure out what those psychics were talking about; I was looking for traumatic events in my childhood, and there really were none. Jayne helped me find the significant, non-traumatic events that formed some limiting beliefs and, for the first time I started to understand why thinking big wasn't working for me.

Jayne helped me locate three significant parts of my life that combined to establish, confirm and lock in a specific limiting belief that really was holding me back; a belief that I never even knew existed. Let me share the stories with you.

For me, the belief system that was validated began when I was two years old. I had an operation on my right eye and every day for five years I wore a patch over my left eye to strengthen the right eye.

I don't have any trauma around that. I remember the patch as part of life. I don't have any negative memories around it. However, it turns out that I not only remember the patch, I remember every minute detail about the patch. I remember what it looked like and smelled like. I remember what it sounded like to take the paper off the back. I remember the pattern on the patch. I remember what the box looked like, how many patches were in the box, and where the box was kept. I remember every detail.

When I was in kindergarten and grade one, I would peel the corner of the patch up, because I couldn't see. Whenever I did that, my older sister, teachers, and parents would immediately push the patch back down. So, I just stopped trying to peek through the patch and I dealt with it, seven days a week for five years.

Again, there was no trauma around the patch, I just remember it as part of my life. No big deal, right? Wrong! Turns out, it was a much bigger deal than I ever knew.

Jayne helped me identify two other stories in my life which confirmed and then locked in a specific limiting belief.

Around age eight I was watching TV. An infomercial came on from the Canadian Wildlife Service showing a little educational video explaining the life of a beaver. At the end of the infomercial the announcer said, "For more information about the beaver, contact the Canadian Wildlife Service," and the phone number appeared on the screen. So, I called!

A few days later I received a package in the mail addressed to "Mr. Steven Lowell." I thought that was the coolest day of my life! Not only did I get mail for the first time, but it was addressed to Mr. Steven Lowell! How cool is that?

Inside the package was a full color brochure with information all about the beaver. So, I thought, "I wonder what other animals they have information on." I called the number again.

Turns out they had information on every animal found in Canada, hundreds of them! I called every day for weeks requesting information on a new animal. Each day I was getting mail, each piece addressed to "Mr. Steve Lowell." It was awesome!

About a week into the process, I noticed a TV advertisement for Jamaica as a vacation destination. At the end of the commercial the voice said, "For more information about Jamaica, contact the Jamaican embassy." The phone number came on the screen. What's a guy to do? I called the number of course!

A few days later I received two pieces of mail, one from the Canadian Wildlife Service and one from the Jamaican embassy. Both of them addressed to "Mr. Steven Lowell."

I remember thinking, I don't know what an embassy is, but I know that they'll send you things. I wondered if there were more embassies. I opened the phone book (if you were born before 1972, you'll know what that is!).

In the middle pages of the phone book I struck gold! It turned out that there were dozens of embassies in Ottawa; I began calling. I called one per day and requested information about their country, and they were happy to send it!

Before long I was receiving two pieces of mail every single day, all addressed to Mr. Steven Lowell. I stockpiled all this content in my bedroom until I was running out of room.

It was summertime. School was out and I had lots of time to fill. I started thinking about what I should do with all this information, then the idea struck. I gathered up all my packets of information, placed them in my little pull-wagon and launched my first business going door to door asking people if they would like to buy some information.

The full-colored pieces sold best. Then I'd go home and order more. I sold the pieces for 10 cents or maybe a quarter per piece. Remember, this was 1970ish. For an eight-year-old boy in 1970, 25 cents was an enormous amount of money. I was raking it in!

One day my mom noticed the piles of mail in my room and in my wagon. She asked me about it, and I told her what I was doing. She asked me if I thought it was fair to take money for something I hadn't paid for. She didn't really give it much thought. There was no anger or judgment in her words, it was just a simple question asked in passing. In fact, she has no memory of these events. But she was my mom and she was right because to my eight-year-old mind, my parents were always right. I hadn't given that question any thought before she asked it. I hadn't paid for this information and it was probably unfair of me to be taking money for it, so I closed down the operation, discarded or gave away the rest of the information I had accumulated and went on with my life.

Once again, there has never been any trauma around those events. In fact, I'm quite proud of my entrepreneurial prowess as an eight-year-old.

Looking back on that time now, I can see where I could have justified the enterprise. Even if I didn't pay for the inventory, there is value in the door-to-door delivery, my time as an entrepreneur, curating and managing the inventory and wear and tear on my wagon. All these factors made the enterprise a legitimate business. But as an eight-year-old, I had no concept of these things. I didn't pay for the inventory and so I shouldn't take money for it. No big deal, right? Wrong! This too turned out to be a much bigger deal than I ever thought.

After I shared this story with Jayne, she took me forward to my teenage years.

There was no specific event that came to my memory from my teenage years. What did come up was a more general state of being during high school.

I hated everything about high school. In fact, I hated everything in life when I was in high school. My self-image was that of a greasy-haired nerd who wasn't good at anything, and I blamed everything and everyone at school for it all.

What I hated most about high school was that I had grown tired of following everyone else's rules as to when I had to show up, when I was allowed to leave, when I had to take lunch and where I had to be each hour of the day. I did, however comply with it all, a pattern that would become apparent years later in my life. I showed up on time, never skipped a class, never left early and did everything I was being forced to do, but I resented every minute of it, failed many of the subjects and left the minute I was allowed to do so.

When Jayne explored these three experiences in my life with me, she found that several limiting beliefs had been established; she was able to connect those beliefs to behavioral patterns that were keeping me stuck.

From my experience with the eye patch, I formulated a belief system that was supported and galvanized by the other two experiences. It was a belief system that was holding me back in every area of my life.

The main belief system stemming from those experiences was that certain things in my life had to be tolerated because somebody said I had to tolerate them. In each case, whenever there was instruction, or even a suggestion made by someone whom I perceived was in a position of authority, I would accept that instruction or suggestion as truth and I would unconsciously comply. My self-image was such that almost everyone was in a position of perceived authority.

The scariest thing about all of this is that I never knew it existed. I was completely and totally blind to it all until Jayne put the evidence in front of me. She was able to point out myriad things in my life that I was tolerating because I thought they were law.

I realized in my personal life as well as in my business, I needed to ask myself some important questions; what am I tolerating? What might I actually be able to change?

With Jayne's guidance, the first major realization I reached was that I was tolerating my fees.

Every time I would quote a fee for my services, the prospect would tell me what they were willing to pay, and I accepted that as truth. I was always dropping my fees to the point where I often gave my services away just so I might have a chance at future business from this person.

As an example of how devastating my limiting beliefs were to my life and my business, let me introduce you to Kristen.

Kristen and
My Bouncing Fees

I had received a phone call from Kristen, an acquaintance from a few events at which I had spoken.

Kristen was in a bit of a panic because she had invested almost six figures with one trainer to teach her how to sell her coaching from the platform when she spoke at events. This coach had helped her create a presentation she'd been using for the better part of a year and her sales results were dismal. She called me asking for my help.

I helped Kristen redesign her entire presentation for an upcoming speaking engagement at which she needed to make some sales.

After the speaking engagement Kristen texted me with the results. Not only did she generate $69,000 in revenue on the spot, but she got booked for three additional speaking engagements; solely because of the presentation I helped her craft.

Great news, right? Until I tell you how much I charged her for my help.

When Kristen called me, she had mentioned how much she had originally invested in her former coach and she expressed concern about investing much more. I took her words to heart and I charged her a total of $500.

Now, Kristen didn't overtly negotiate my fees or try to get me to lower them. It was just her suggestion that she was concerned about investing that triggered my limiting belief and pulled me into my pattern of giving in to what I perceived as the truth. I tolerated a ridiculous fee for a service that had tremendous value to Kristen.

I was thrilled to be able to help Kristen in this way. I was, and still am proud to have been part of Kristen's success. This event with Kristen caused me to think about my fees and to again attempt to think bigger. So, I raised my fees until I received objections about my fees from prospects and clients. I followed my own limiting pattern and dropped them again.

Thinking Big in Hollywood

In January of 2015 I started dating Jayne. We decided to join forces and build a business together. Over the next year we supported each other in our respective businesses as we slowly merged our businesses into one. Then I decided we were ready to think bigger, so we set our sights on Los Angeles. I wanted to hold an event in LA, and we decided to make that happen.

We had previously run a small event in LA which turned out okay. We had about 25 people, most of them friends and existing clients, and we generated a small amount of revenue from that event. So, we thought doing it again would be easy, and this time we'd think bigger! We'd aim for 200 people at the event.

We set the date, secured the venue and started promoting.

In very short order it was becoming clear that we were not going to have even close to 200 people at this event. In fact, we had done everything we could think of and we had four registrations.

We tried everything. We invested in marketing "experts" who were happy to take our money but were not able to generate a single viable lead for our event.

Through some social media channels, I connected with a guy named Levi. Levi was an expert in filling events, and he told me he was so confident that he could fill our event that he would fill it for free. I would have to commit to spending some money on Facebook ads, but he would engage his entire staff and do all the work for free just to prove that he could do it. His hope was that we would then engage him afterwards to fill more events. I was excited.

Levi put one condition on his offer. We would have to move the event to any city in the world other than Los Angeles.

He told me he could predict within a reasonable margin of error how many would attend any event in almost any city in the world except LA. There are too many variables in LA to predict such an outcome.

The problem was that we had already committed to the venue in LA for 200 people and it was all non-refundable since we were less than a month out. Moving the event was not an option we could face.

Levi agreed to follow through under the agreement that I would not hold him to the final estimated turnout. He told me if we invested $10,000 on Facebook ads, we would have roughly 300 registrations. We would hire someone to confirm each of these registrations by phone two or three days before the event. Levi predicted that roughly 200 people would confirm. Of those, roughly 100 people would show up. But that was anywhere else in the world. In LA, he said 100 people might show up, none of them might show up; that's just LA.

We proceeded.

We invested $6,000 in Facebook ads, all of which were created and managed by Levi's team. Just over 200 people registered as Levi predicted based on the $6,000 ad spend.

We hired someone to make the follow up calls according to Levi's process, about 150 people confirmed. So far, Levi was pretty much bang on with his predictions.

We were able to lower our commitment with the venue a little and we set up the room for 75 attendees. We ordered lunch, printed the materials and name tags and rented sound equipment, all designed for an audience of 75 with some flexibility to extend it to 85 or even 100 if we needed to.

At 9:00 AM the next day, we began delivering our event to an audience of 12 people, eight of whom were original registrants or friends of ours.

The LA event cost us tens of thousands of dollars and nothing ever came of it. By that time, I had had enough of thinking bigger; it cost too much!

APPLYING A DEEP THOUGHT STRATEGY

Our attempt at an event in Los Angeles cost us tens of thousands of dollars because our entire strategy was built around thinking big.

A deep thought strategy would have revealed inherent challenges with an event in Los Angeles that remained hidden from us because we didn't think deep enough:

- We had only a handful of influencers in LA and we assumed that because they liked us, they would help us fill a room. Beyond some commission on ticket sales, we provided no reason for our contacts in LA to help us, and they didn't.

- LA provides more options for people to invest their time and money than almost any other city in the world. We gave them no compelling reason to select our event over other options.

- The competitive environment in LA is not the same as it is in Ottawa. Ottawa has only a handful of people who do anything even similar to what I do, but LA has thousands of them. In addition, people in LA have access to some of the biggest names in the world, and there are events held every single day by one or more of those big names. Our event competes with those names.

By hosting an event in LA, we fell into the thinking big illusion once again. Had we applied a deep thought strategy, we would have:

- Found out what our influencers needed most and made sure they were able to obtain that by helping us fill the room

- Taught our influencers how to present our event to their contacts as a solution to a problem they never knew they had, rather than just another event by an outsider promising the same things as their local gurus

- Made clear the cost of not attending the event in a currency relevant to the LA audience

Jayne's Mindset Magic

One of the limiting beliefs that Jayne uncovered within me was a belief that wealth was temporary for me. Because of certain life circumstances, any money that came into my life was immediately extracted. It was normal for me to earn some money, get paid; and within hours or even minutes it would be taken away from me by multiple sources in my life. It was a pattern that had been established years prior and had become one of those realities I accepted as truth.

During the time I was working with Jayne on my belief systems, my friend Bob and I held our final Your Stage event. At the last session a group of our regular attendees had taken up a small collection for Bob and me as a gesture of appreciation. We each were given $300 cash.

Later that same day I was having a phone call with Jayne and she asked me about that $300. When I told her it had been taken by one of the many sources which routinely absolved me of my money, she gave me strict instructions that I was to follow immediately. I was to go to the bank, withdraw $300 and keep it in my pocket no matter who demanded it from me. So, I did.

Jayne then told me to triple my fees. I was petrified. I knew that no one would pay those fees and I was afraid I'd never get another client. But I complied.

The next time someone asked me about my fees I was almost unable to say the words. But I did and guess what happened; the prospect objected. But I stood my ground with my fees. I didn't budge. I lost the sale.

Losing that sale was significant. It taught me that I can lose a sale and still survive. It was the first time I didn't cave. For once

I didn't give in to someone else's view because they said so. It put me in a different category. To that one person, I was the best, really expensive and unattainable at the price he was willing to pay. My first baby step.

It was tough. I lost a few deals because I believed I was worth the higher rate and I refused to compromise. Then, something amazing happened. Someone paid my higher fee. My second baby step.

After three months of working with Jayne I had doubled my business. I purchased my first luxury car, a 2013 Mercedes C350, my next baby step.

Jayne had such an amazing impact on my life in that short time. I started to realize that thinking bigger was never going to work for me until I did something else first; I needed to start thinking deeper. Then maybe, just maybe, bigger would come.

Jayne had officially changed my life. So, I did what any good client would do; I married her!

REPUTATION
AND EXPERT INSIGHTS

Over the next two years I worked hard at changing the way I thought about things. Changing my limiting beliefs was difficult for me; I kept slipping into my old belief patterns. Fortunately for me, I had Jayne to keep me focused.

Our business started to grow very quickly. I kept increasing my fees and people were paying them. I found myself working less to obtain new clients. Referrals increased and my reputation was changing; people were seeking me out, asking me to speak at their events.

I had been a member of the Canadian Association of Professional Speakers (CAPS) for several years and I been able to establish a presence within that world. In 2017 I was elected National President-Elect and I would serve as National President in 2018.

By that time, I had earned the "Certified Speaking Professional" (CSP) designation (the highest designation in the professional speaking world) and I was getting some attention from my target audience because of these credentials.

At the same time, Jayne was establishing her presence as "The 7-Figure Mindset Mentor" and she was filling her own calendar with clients from around the globe.

I knew that my new credentials and all the exposure they had provided certainly helped our business, but there was something else at work; something that was driving our business upward and something that I couldn't identify.

Of course, I was thrilled about our rate of growth and our success, but I became curious as to why it was happening. I didn't feel like I was doing that much differently from what I had always done, and yet we were getting entirely different results. As exciting as that was, it was also scary because I didn't know why it was happening, which made it feel temporary to me. I wanted to understand what had changed so I could reproduce it by design.

I traced my steps back to that experience with the Christmas decorations. I was looking for changes in my process, strategy or behavior; anything that would help me understand what had directly influenced our success so I could do it deliberately.

I could find small changes in our approach to serving clients, holding events and other things, but there was nothing glaringly obvious that had changed. Then I found it!

When I reminded myself about my experience with the Christmas decorations and my aspiration to be "The very best, really expensive, if you can even get him," it occurred to me that I was looking for the change in the wrong places. I was looking for changes in what I was doing, I should have been looking for changes in my reputation.

As I looked back and traced my journey through the lens of what others were saying about me, I discovered that my reputation had gone through multiple states. As I reviewed my experiences, I could clearly map out my path.

Since then I have field-tested my theory by helping others recognize their own position on their own journey in terms of their reputation. I've validated the approach by teaching others to do exactly what we did within the context of their own business.

I have since formalized that journey into a series of models which I teach as part of my programs. These models help entrepreneurs to think deeper before thinking bigger by deploying a deep thought strategy to move their reputation to the point where they become, what I call "THE One," the only logical choice.

This transition to "THE One" happens when a deep thought strategy is deployed to reveal something I call "expert Insights." Finding the expert insights is where the deep thought comes in.

Using your expert insights deliberately and tactically is where the strategy comes in.

The rest of this book is dedicated to helping apply your own deep thought strategy to find your own expert insights so you can properly prepare yourself for not only thinking big, but actually DOING big. It all starts with, what I call, your "Repumeter™."

PART TWO

THE REPUMETER™

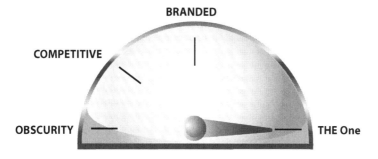

THE REPUMETER™

Throughout my career I have noticed that so many experts struggle to position themselves as unique in their field. Of course, the challenge is that very few of them actually ARE unique, even though most think they are – this is a big problem for those who try to think big. As we have seen, thinking bigger can be costly if it means more of the same. This means that you need to get past your own ego and put something in place that actually makes you appear to be different. (Remember Brian, the tennis instructor?)

I will often ask people the question; what makes you different? In almost every single case the answer contains one or more of these things:

- Tenure (I have been in the business 35 years)
- Service (We customize our service, spend more time with clients)
- Solution (I have a unique approach, my three pillars to this or my four secrets to that)

The problem is none of these three elements are differentiators. When you rely on any or all of these elements, all you are doing is making yourself look and sound exactly like everyone else who does what you do; you're a tennis instructor!

Because of this, standing out can be a challenge. Nevertheless, standing out is what you must do on your way to thinking bigger and playing a bigger game.

Based on my own experience of having gone through this myself, I can clearly see where so many others are going through the exact same thing; they just can't see it any more than I could when I was in the thick of it.

To help my audiences and clients better understand why they are getting stuck, I developed a grid to map out the various states that I went through. I can observe my clients going through these same states and know what causes them to move between the states. I thought if I could demonstrate that I understand what my prospects and audiences are going through, I might position myself as a good choice to help them.

I didn't realize it at the time, but I was thinking deeper, not bigger.

What I came up with was a description of the journey I experienced, and I represent it as the typical journey that I see most entrepreneurs go through. I have since validated this entire process with thousands of people all over the world.

What follows is the typical journey of the speaker, coach, consultant, sales professional and expert of any kind. I call it "The Repumeter™."

The Repumeter™ is a tool that measures the state of your reputation. Looking back on my journey through the Repumeter™ lens, I can pinpoint every step I have made from one state to the next. Meanwhile, the Repumeter™ continues to evolve. I'm now known all over the world as "The Repumeter™ Guy."

This is powerful. We have crashed through the 7-figure barrier by building a strategy around this information. By understanding how you are placed in the minds of your target audience, you can develop a process to position yourself as the known expert in your field, whatever your field is, and then leverage that positioning by crafting your message strategically and delivering your message tactically. It's your deep thought strategy that gets you there.

THE FOUR
REPUMETER™ MILESTONES

Through our professional journey our reputation typically falls into one of four states. Some move from state to state, most just stay where they are.

OBSCURITY

The first state is what I call "Obscurity."

Obscurity means people in your circles don't really know who you are or what you do.

This state can be somewhat deceptive because it's easy to confuse a large circle of connection for a large circle of influence. It's a common misconception that because you're connected to a lot of people, they all know what you do, when in fact, they don't.

You know you are in Obscurity when:

- The phone isn't ringing with referrals or prospective clients
- You go to networking groups or meetings and very few people, if anyone at all, knows who you are. People are not introducing you to others and you find it challenging to get noticed.

- You're operating in your business from a standpoint of need; always trying to figure out where the next contract, or the next speaking gig, or the next customer is coming from
- No one is asking you to speak anywhere
- You're always trying to figure out how you can pay your bills, because you're not making much money and it's all a continual struggle
- Your energy and all your activities are all based on attracting business to you

In the state of Obscurity, you're always asking yourself these questions:

- Why am I not getting referrals?
- Why are people not calling and saying, "I want to work with you?"
- Why is it so hard to close sales?
- Why do I keep losing sales?
- Why am I not getting paid speaking gigs?
- Why are my books, products or services not selling?
- Why are people not signing up for my events?

When I was in this state, if I wasn't at another networking "opportunity," I was creating something new. I always felt that if I just created a new webinar, updated my website, improved my LinkedIn profile, wrote another book or blog post or, put another video on social media someone would notice me!

I thought if I just did more of everything, I would get noticed and be successful. If I thought bigger, did more it would all work out:

"What if I launch the MLM Executive Round Table?"

"What if I hold an event in LA?"

Get the point? (if not, might I suggest that you review "The Origins of Deep Thought Strategy" and "Thinking Big in Hollywood" sections of this book).

We can lock ourselves into the Obscurity state by doing the wrong things or by not doing the right things. Many people get stuck here and never make progress.

I know a lot of people who operate in the Obscurity state forever and never advance beyond that state because they don't know how to make that jump into the Competitive state, let alone the Branded state and beyond.

I believe this is why a high percentage of businesses, particularly speakers, coaches, trainers, authors, and consultants go out of business so quickly and why salespeople struggle to close deals. They get stuck in the state of Obscurity, and they're not in any category. It's exhausting working at this level.

COMPETITIVE

When we stay in business long enough, and people start paying a little bit of attention to us, we come to the state that I call "Competitive."

Competitive means people in your circles have a pretty good idea of what you do, but there's nothing that separates you from everybody else who does what you do. Figuratively, you're a tennis instructor! (See "Deep Thought Strategy at Work")

Even though it's certainly better than Obscurity, all it means is that now you're in the game. It doesn't mean that you're standing head and shoulders above anybody, and it doesn't mean that your business is building momentum. You know you're in the Competitive state when these things are happening:

- You're getting some business, but you're still working hard for it
- You find yourself negotiating your fees so you can get the business before your competitor gets the business
- You might include bonuses or freebies to sweeten the pot a little so you can win the business

- Your sales presentation always seems to come down to price

- Referrals start to come in from time to time, but most of them are exploring other options as well, and you go right back to competing on price or perceived value

- You have an "a" or "an" kind of identity. People refer to you as a noun. You're a coach, you're a speaker, you're a financial advisor, you're a trainer, you're a mortgage broker, you're a real estate agent, you're a consultant, you're a salesperson, you're "a" something. You're in what I call a category of many.

- You may get the very odd request to speak, but the request is usually followed by the words, "We have no budget for speakers."

- You get invited to speak for "exposure," as if the privilege of being in front of their audience is of more value to you than your message is to them.

- People you know hire your competitors to do what you do. If you're a coach, they hire somebody else to coach them. If you're an author, they buy somebody else's books. They hire other consultants, not you, even though they know you exist and you're in the game.

- You may even be mis-branded. People may think they know what you do, but they may not be quite on the mark and pass you over when opportunities present themselves

Between the states of "Obscurity" and "Competitive," your reputation is typically defined through a random branding process where the marketplace defines your reputation because you have not provided any control by which your reputation can be defined.

When I was in this state (and I was in this state for years!), I become badly mis-branded.

I was in the "Competitive" state when I let the market brand me based on their perception. My reputation was based on what people could see:

- He runs a little group called Your Stage
- He's really inexpensive
- He's always around
- He trains speakers (but is not a speaker himself)

The Competitive state is where most people stay forever. They do the same things everybody else does in exactly the same way. They become "tennis instructors."

The State of Competitive for Speakers

I see this very often with speakers. Jayne and I travel the world, we go to many summits, many professional speaker association conventions and we see a lot of speakers. There are many magnificent speakers. They are skilled and talented, and yet so many of them look the same as everybody else. Why is that?

Unless one of them had something very specific that targeted a direct need for me, I've probably forgotten most of them because they blend in and look the same as every other speaker. They get on the stage with a whole bunch of PowerPoint slides, they tell some stories, they make me chuckle from time to time, and when they leave the stage I walk away thinking, that was really good. Yet, the message drifts away from my awareness.

It's not that they're poor speakers. It's that they're locking themselves in at this Competitive state by doing what every other speaker does.

The State of Competitive for Sales Professionals

When a salesperson represents a company which is in the Repumeter™ state of Competitive, they compete against more than just the solutions of their competitors; they compete against several competitive factors including the sales skills of their competition, existing relationships between the prospect and other providers, their company's reputation, history and brand awareness just to name a few.

When a salesperson meets a prospect for the first time, they often need to sell so much more than their solution; they often need to sell their entire company profile and establish a relationship before the prospect even considers looking seriously at the solution.

Even if the salesperson provides an outstanding sales presentation, chances are superb that that presentation includes much of the above in order to establish credibility, forge a relationship, demonstrate solutions and begin any negotiations; and that is the problem. The salesperson looks like every other salesperson. That's the nature of the state of Competitive.

The State of Competitive for Coaches

According to the International Coach Federation (ICF) website, as of April 2017 there were 30,000 members of the federation. An October 2019 internet search revealed that the ICF estimates there are over 53,000 coaches.

According to marketresearch.com, as of February 2018 the personal coaching industry topped $1 billion in the US alone; there are A LOT of coaches out there!

Coaches are in a super competitive space, and to stand out as a coach is extremely difficult when doing it the old-fashioned way: competing against solutions.

I know hundreds of coaches of all types. Hundreds of times I have observed coaches on the platform sharing their unique solutions.

One after the other, they present their systems, processes and tools; each one positioning themselves as another tennis instructor (See "Deep Thought Strategy at Work").

Whenever I ask a coach, "What makes you different?" though the words vary, the answer is always the same: years of experience, level of service and unique approach. On occasion they will use their credentials as a differentiator, "I am ICF Certified." So are more than 30,000 other coaches!

Of all the professions I have encountered, coaches are among those who struggle to stand out the most. And it's mainly because so many are adding speaking to their marketing activities and promotion efforts, and they so often get in front of an audience and lock themselves into the Competitive state because of how they present themselves.

The good news for you as a coach is this: as competitive as the space is, you have the opportunity to demonstrate a unique knowledge of your clients' world that no other coach can claim. While all the other coaches are waving their hands in the air yelling, "Look at me, I'm the same as everyone else," you have the opportunity to capture your prospects' attention by putting the focus of your conversation on them and the problem they never even knew they had. That's what your deep thought strategy does.

BRANDED

The next state on the Repumeter™ is what I call, "Branded."

At the "Branded" stage, people in your circles know who you are and what you do, and there is beginning to be something noticeable about you, but they may not be able to define exactly what that is.

At this stage you begin to see an increase in referrals, though prospects will still be shopping around. You'll still need to compete with others for business, but your name comes up among the first recommendations by others.

Typically, your referrals have some idea of what your fees might be, or at least what ballpark you play in regarding fees.

They're not ready to sign on the dotted line until after they have done some checking, but you'll notice that they may attempt to negotiate a little less, and they may be ready to pay higher fees with a little convincing from you.

You may still negotiate your terms, but you're not as concerned about survival and you're at the point where you can be just a little more selective about your clientele.

"Branded" is an important spot on your Repumeter™ for two reasons:

   1. It's a tentative condition that can easily dissolve causing your reputation to revert back to Competitive

2. It's the spot where your name begins to become associated with something other than your title

Branded can be a tentative condition because your circles are starting to notice you a little more, which means they will watch you through a more critical lens. Their expectations will increase, they will evaluate what they see and hear more critically, and they'll seek to validate (or invalidate) your status.

If the perceived reality does not match the expectations, your reputation can quickly drop back to Competitive and this can be damaging because you can actually become known as one who was not able to measure up to the reputation.

This state on your Repumeter™ can also be a launching pad to bigger and better things. For that to happen, your name needs to be re-associated from your title to something else.

As previously mentioned, while navigating past Obscurity and into Competitive, your name is primarily associated with your title. You're known as "a" something or "an" something. This association pigeonholes you into a category of many. You become one of a larger population; you're a tennis instructor.

This makes thinking bigger dangerous because at these stages all you have to offer, at least in the minds of your circles, is more of the same.

Once you enter the Branded state there's an opportunity for your name to be re-associated. This happens because of the increased scrutiny that occurs once you reach this status. There are two specific criteria against which you will be evaluated by your circles. For you to leverage your position at Branded you'll need to make sure to reach or exceed expectations for two criteria and ultimately have your name associated with one or both:

1. The results that you provide

2. The experience you provide

When this re-association happens, and your name becomes associated with either or both of these criteria, you have secured your position at the Branded stage. You're not yet ready to think bigger, but you're beginning to prepare the field.

You'll recall Kristen (See "Kristen and My Bouncing Fees") whom I coached and who then rocked the stage to the tune of $69,000 in revenue from that one speaking engagement. During that same presentation she received two standing ovations. The moment she got off the stage Kristen got in front of the camera and sent me an excited testimonial about the two standing ovations. I placed that testimonial on my website and YouTube channel because it was a nice little testimonial, but I had no idea of the power that testimonial would later provide.

After that testimonial went live, I received a few (not many, but a few) emails from other speakers asking if I could help them get standing ovations too. I realized that I might actually be on to something. Maybe I could get known as the guy who helps you get standing ovations.

I reached out to everyone I could think of with whom I had done any work at all to see if I could get more testimonials just like Kristen's. I found a mix of results that were being achieved, but there was no specific pattern to them that I could discern. I knew I wanted my name associated with some kind of a result, but the results were all different; I couldn't find a pattern to cling to.

Then the pattern emerged.

As I trained more and more speakers, the pattern that emerged was speakers generating revenue when they spoke. They would sell more books, get more clients and higher speaking fees.

Over time I collected multiple testimonials confirming the results my clients were getting and eventually my name became associated with making money from the front of the room.

I had already established a reputation for providing an outstanding experience through my Your Stage events, but I wanted to ensure that my name became associated with both outstanding results and an outstanding experience.

Over time, it worked. I had controlled the branding well enough that I became known for holding extremely high-value events and helping speakers sell from the platform. It was a good position to be in. Now, here is a big word of caution!

At this stage you will be inspired to think bigger. You'll have the confidence to launch into something bigger and you'll be willing to invest because your belief in yourself and your business will be strong. Don't do it! Not yet! You're not ready! Let me explain.

If you reach the Branded stage on your Repumeter™ it's because you are good at what you do and you're getting recognized for that. But that doesn't make you different, it only makes you better. "Better" is not the same as different.

Remember Brian the tennis instructor? (See "Deep Thought Strategy at Work") Let's review the three lessons from Brian because they become applicable for you right now.

Let's explore these one at a time because your next steps to developing your deep thought strategy depend on you grasping this concept.

1. You don't need to be different from everyone else who does what you do, you only need to appear to be different.

Notice that there is no reference to being "better" than everyone else who does what you do, it's about appearing to be different.

If you reach the Branded stage on your Repumeter™, it's most likely because your name has become associated with the results you provide and/or the experience you provide. Both of these could point to "better" and not "different." Better is subjective; open to interpretation and opinion. Different is less so. Though better is a very good thing; your objective is to appear to be different, even if you're not.

2. You appear to be different by changing the language you use about yourself.

By changing the language you use about yourself, you teach the world what language to use when they speak about you. This is called controlled branding. By controlling how others speak about you, you can guide the conversation towards what makes you appear to be different. There is a specific process to help you do that. It's all part of your deep thought strategy.

Stay with me here, we're going to explore how you control the conversation and make yourself appear to be different by using something called your expert insights.

3. Your message must be easy to understand and easily repeated.

The message that you share with the world needs to be more than information; it must also be a signature. It needs to be something that people can not only repeat but also attach your name to. Your message needs to have meaning to them beyond the message itself; it must be directly applicable to their lives – that's what expert insights are.

We'll be exploring the concept of expert insights in detail. For now, what you need to know is when your name becomes associated with your own expert insights, that's when you begin to move to the fourth stage on your Repumeter™, "THE One."

THE ONE

The fourth state on the Repumeter™ is what I call "THE One." It's the ultimate. This is exactly where you want to be.

At THE One, you are no longer in a category of many, you are no longer in a category of a few, you are now a category of one, the only logical choice.

You know you're at this stage when these things are happening:

- You no longer have to compete for business. Clients come looking for you because they already know they want you.

- You set whatever fees you like, and the only prospects who don't pay them are those who can't afford them, and you're okay with that

- You get to pick and choose with whom you work. You can turn away any business that doesn't meet your prerequisites.

- You work from a position of passion instead of necessity

- You are known as 'the very best, really expensive, if they can even get you'

- People begin to emulate you. They look to you for answers because they want what you have.

- Your work is recognized and implemented across your circles. Your circle of connection becomes your circle of influence.

In this state your energy becomes more about working in your passion than about attracting business. You start to operate from a position of being creative and being of service. You don't have to worry about generating money as a full-time job. You don't need to work as hard to get new clients. You can create, write, and deliver; you can build and connect, doing all those things that generate significant momentum in your business. You now have more time to devote to other aspects of your business, your family, or other communities in which you participate or causes you support.

Your reputation begins to spread quickly as others share the impact you have had with their own circles of influence, thus escalating the visibility of your reputation and your work.

Your work is recognized in places you have never presented.

I first had a glimpse of this state when Jayne and I were in Cape Town for the national convention of the Professional Speakers Association of Southern Africa. I had spoken three times during the event.

The first day was a special day for local corporate delegates. I presented my Repumeter™ concept which I normally draw on a flip chart. It's a graphic which looks like a speedometer with the four stages located on the arc. I always present this using flip charts instead of slides so I can interact with the graphic; it's just the way I like to present.

After I presented, I moved the flip chart out of the way and placed it against a wall where it would not be a distraction for the following speakers over the next two days. The flip chart remained there, untouched with my hand-drawn graphic of the Repumeter™ facing outward.

On the final day of the event, someone I had never met walked up to me, introduced himself, pointed to the flip chart and said, "Hey Steve, isn't that your reputation thing?"

I knew then that I had something that not only made me appear to be different, but it was memorable and repeatable; it became one of my signature pieces.

Before we move on, let me ask you these two questions:

1. Do you know where you are on your own Repumeter™?

2. Are you exactly where you want and need to be?

Hold your answers for now, I'll come back to this later.

The Repumeter™ is part of my expert insights and has since become the foundation of my deep thought strategy which now prepares me to think big. Thinking big is no longer an illusion for me, it is now part of a deep thought strategy that has taken and continues to take Jayne and I all over the world.

What follows is the rest of my own expert insights and how they apply to you. You'll need to understand these concepts to execute your deep thought strategy and find your own expert insights. Then we'll explore the steps you need to take to craft your expert insights into a powerful message so you can be prepared for thinking big.

INFLUENCE, IMPACT AND OUTCOME

Your position on your Repumeter™ has direct implications in three general business outcomes: influence, impact and income.

The more you advance along the Repumeter™, the more influence your work will have because you'll be serving more people. The more people you are able to influence, the more impact your work will have through the collective influence of those people. The more impact your work has through your extended influence, the more valuable your work becomes, which manifests itself in higher income.

Pretty straightforward, right? But let's take a look at how your place on your own Repumeter™ impacts this process.

Operating in the Obscurity State

If you are operating in the state of Obscurity where those in your circles don't know what you do, how much influence are you likely to have? The answer is little or none.

By extension, if you have little or no influence you have little or no impact. It's easy to see how this situation is not likely to result in a high level of income.

When Jayne and I tried to launch our event in Los Angeles, we overestimated our level of influence. Though our combined circle of connection (mostly social media connections) in that area totaled maybe a few hundred, our actual circle of influence was next to nil.

Because our Repumeter™ position in LA was Obscurity, we had no influence which resulted in no attendees (impact) and so we lost a lot of money (income).

Scale this situation to your entire business and you can see why being in the state of Obscurity is not exactly a recipe for wealth.

OPERATING IN
THE COMPETITIVE STATE

As you move along your Repumeter™ path and enter the state of Competitive where people in your circles have a pretty good idea of what you do, but there's nothing that separates you from everybody else who does what you do, things begin to change, but only a little!

In this state you are slowly beginning to migrate your circle of connection over to your circle of influence by doing business with them and increasing your presence. This means you now have a little more influence than you did at Obscurity, but you have to work for it because you are competing with others who do what you do, at least, in the minds of your circles.

Because you are now at least visible to your circles, and doing business with them, you have more influence. By extension this means that you are having more of an impact and, therefore earning more income. But you're still at the bottom of the scale in all three outcomes as compared to the other two positions on the Repumeter™: Branded and THE One.

During the entire Your Stage experience I can see now that I was struggling through the Competitive state, trying to claw my way up to Branded. Of course, I didn't know it at the time.

The whole time I thought I was leveraging Your Stage as a branding and positioning opportunity; I was blind to the fact that I was being randomly branded as something I never intended: a speaker-coach who is not very successful and who runs very small events. (See "How Thinking Big Kept Me and My Business Small").

Your Stage was a great event. It provided exceptional value and an outstanding experience. Because of this I was elevating my influence and having an impact. I was even seeing a slight increase in income, but not much!

I was doing business and I was surviving, but just barely. I had only enough influence to create enough impact that I could get clients if I made the right deal. But I was nowhere near where I needed or wanted to be on the income scale. That's what happens in the state of Competitive on the Repumeter™.

During these first two states (Obscurity and Competitive) you use more time and effort and achieve fewer results.

Operating in
the Branded State

When you cross the line to the Branded state and start to become known for the results and experience you provide, you begin to see a significant change in your outcomes.

The Branded state is where people in your circles know who you are and what you do, and there is beginning to be something noticeable about you. People may not be able to define exactly what that is; you just seem to be more visible than some others.

You'll notice a change in behavior within your circles as more people transition from your circle of connection to your circle of influence. This happens because your circles are checking you out. They're seeing things or hearing things about you that make them curious and they want to see if you're the real deal or not.

That's why this can be a tentative state. Your circles are seeking to validate your reputation which means you have temporary influence. This gives you a chance to engage people, have a positive impact and welcome them into your circle of influence. The problem is you may not recognize this is what's happening. You may misconstrue the added attention for success, but it's not. It's an opportunity to position yourself for success, but it's an opportunity that can be easily missed.

When I tried to merge Your Stage with The Chamber of Commerce (See "Your Stage: More Thinking Bigger") I can see now that I was in the process of stepping beyond the Repumeter™ state of Competitive into the state of Branded within my circles.

Everyone in the Your Stage crowd knew who I was and what I did, and Your Stage was the experience I provided that made me appear to be different. Some were starting to get results from working with me and were just starting to share those results through their testimonials; the conversation was changing. My name was beginning to become associated with those results as well as with the Your Stage experience.

Because of my promotion of the Your Stage event to the Chamber of Commerce, most people in the Chamber knew who I was and what I did, and my invitation to join us at Your Stage made me appear to be a little different. I was hoping that when they all came to Your Stage, they would have an outstanding experience and that would bring them into my circle of influence. As you now know, that didn't happen.

Many of the Chamber of Commerce attendees walked over to check out Your Stage with the intention of joining us only if what they had heard and seen about me and the Your Stage event was validated. When only eight people showed up at Your Stage, the hype around me and Your Stage was not validated and my position at Branded was lost within the Chamber of Commerce as they slipped out of my circle of influence back into my circle of connection. I lost any opportunity for influence that may have existed.

I became acutely aware that I had overestimated my influence within the Your Stage crowd, and I became painfully aware that I had squandered any shred of influence I may have had with the Chamber of Commerce. My Branded position slipped away, and I became known as just another guy trying to think big. I was a tennis instructor once again.

The Branded state of the Repumeter™ is not a locked-in position. It's a transitional opportunity for you to change the association of your name from a category of many to a category of a few. Miss this opportunity and you further anchor yourself in the Competitive state until the next opportunity comes along, if it ever does.

Once you're at the Branded position and your name becomes securely associated with the results you provide and the experience you provide, it's easy to become complacent. This exposes you to the risk of losing your position as new connections join your circle of influence and validate your stature. You must consistently leverage your influence to create meaningful and significant impact in order to generate acceptable revenue.

With each step along the Repumeter™ path comes the temptation to think bigger, and with it the increasing risk of falling prey to the "think big illusion." At no state is the risk higher than at the Branded state because you have much more to lose, and you're not quite ready for thinking bigger.

It's at this point where thinking deeper becomes most mission critical. This is where your deep thought strategy sets your direction towards the next state and prepares you to scale your business by thinking bigger.

Operating in "THE One" state

Luckily, there is another opportunity available. That opportunity is to move past the Branded state and into the state of "THE One."

Simply put, this is the state where you have maximum influence because your circle of influence is large and, to them you are the only logical choice. This means you have the opportunity for significant impact and with it, significant income.

In the spring of 2017, the Global Speakers Federation (GSF) was hosting the Global Speaker Summit in Auckland, New Zealand and I was selected to speak.

Several years before I had worked with a client from Auckland named Sally. Sally had a huge story and she struggled to be accepted as a professional speaker in the United States. I had helped her with that struggle, and she became a very powerful connection for me.

Over the years she had referred many clients to me, because in Sally's eyes I was THE One.

Sally had always told Jayne and me, if we were ever to make it to Auckland, she would host an event for us so her own clients and colleagues could experience my training. Sally held true to her word.

Because Sally held the Repumeter™ position of THE One within her own circle of influence in Auckland (and beyond), she had enough influence to put 18 of her top clients into a room, each paying $1,000 out of their own pockets all to see Jayne and me for just one day.

When I started the program, I asked two questions of the audience:

The first question was, "Put up your hand if you know what to expect today."

Not a single hand went up. Everyone in that room paid us $1,000 out of their own pocket without knowing a single thing about me or what was going to happen that day.

The second question was, "Why on earth would you do that?"

The answer to that question was simple; "Because Sally said we needed to!"

Now THAT'S influence!

I delivered a full-day workshop for this group and by lunch time we had 10 paid registrations to an $8,000 group coaching program. We generated almost $100,000 in business that one day all because of an influencer who was THE One within her circle of influence.

When you operate in the state of THE One, everything about your business and your life becomes easier. Once you apply your deep thought strategy and position yourself as THE One, you're ready to think bigger, MUCH bigger!

PART THREE

DEEP THOUGHT
STRATEGY
PREREQUISITES

There are three prerequisites that must be achieved before your reputation can move along the Repumeter™ in preparation for your deep thought strategy and thinking bigger. You must achieve all three prerequisites. Without all three, your Repumeter™ progress will be stalled and your deep thought strategy will never be properly assembled. Let's explore those now.

PREREQUISITE #1:
Outstanding Client Results and an Outstanding Experience

The bottom line on this first prerequisite is: if you're not able to get outstanding results for your clients and provide them an outstanding experience, you simply need to get better at what you do. Master your craft, learn more, and do whatever it is you need to do to achieve outstanding results for those clients by providing an outstanding experience. Without this, your reputation may move across the Repumeter™, but you will never withstand the scrutiny that occurs at the Branded state, if you ever even get there.

If you're not sure if your clients are getting outstanding results, or if you're not even sure how to measure that, I recommend that you speak with your clients. Let them define what outstanding results or experience means to them and do what you must to make certain they achieve those results or have that experience.

No matter what field you're in, there is a way to define outstanding results and experience.

It could be as simple as being responsive and reliable.

Outstanding Results:
A Mortgage Agent

In 2017 Jayne and I purchased some property on which we planned to build our dream home. As a new couple, both self-employed, it was difficult to find suitable financing at a reasonable interest rate.

We struggled through multiple mortgage agents over the course of two years. Each of them provided a great initial experience, but then became completely unresponsive. They stopped returning phone calls and texts, they missed deadlines, they made promises they never kept and each one either completely dropped off the face of the earth or came back to us with an impossible deal. We were searching for a mortgage agent who would show us a little professional courtesy.

Then we found Jeff.

Not only did Jeff provide an exceptional first experience, he kept us informed every step of the way, returned every single phone call and text within minutes and within about a week he found us the money we needed at a very reasonable interest rate.

Any one of those other agents could have done what Jeff did, but he was the only one who was professional enough to see the job through. That was both an outstanding result and an outstanding experience for us.

Since that time, we have told many of our local contacts about all these mortgage agents. Guess which one we always recommend.

Outstanding Experience:
A Training Company

In 1994 I decided I wanted to be in sales in the corporate training world. I selected the training company with the best reputation in the city; it was easy to find. I asked around and the same name kept coming up over and over again; a technical computer training company called NetVision.

Luckily, a colleague of mine had just started working there. He gave me the name and contact information of the owner of NetVision, Anil (Yes, the same Anil that would help me with Your Stage almost 20 years later). I wrote to Anil and asked for an interview; I got one.

My interview did not go as planned. I was very confident at first, but my confidence faded quickly as Anil fired question after question, most of which I did not answer well. I was caught off guard; I didn't get the job.

But something else did happen during that interview. I was in awe of the quality of the entire experience. From the time I was greeted at reception on my way in, to the time I was wished a good day on my way out, I was blown away at the level of professionalism and quality of the entire environment. I decided I wasn't finished pursuing this job. This place had the reputation of being the best, and I wanted to work there.

For three months I hounded Anil. I wrote letters, left voice messages, dropped in, all to no avail. Then one day I decided I would call early in the morning before the receptionists arrived. Anil answered the phone. I was able to persuade Anil to give me a chance. I had no idea what I was in for.

Over the next year I learned what it meant to provide an outstanding experience.

As an employee, the experience was highly challenging, not always enjoyable, but valuable beyond measure. To me, Anil was a mentor, a boss and soon become a friend. I knew I was getting an education, and I took advantage of the whole experience.

One of the things I learned from Anil was the importance of providing an outstanding client experience. While other training companies may have delivered acceptable quality training, they would never match the quality and experience NetVision provided.

First, Anil only hired the very best instructors and paid them accordingly. These instructors were sought-after by other training companies. Anil provided such an outstanding experience for them, they stayed with him.

The classrooms contained only the most current equipment and top-of-the-line furniture.

Clients were welcomed each morning with fresh coffee and donuts and served coffee and cookies in the afternoon. When they completed their training, their certificates were mounted on high-quality, wooden mounts.

The entire operation was masterfully designed to provide an outstanding client experience during every minute of their training. It was easy to see why NetVision had the reputation it did.

NetVision's reputation was based on the experience they provided their clients. Though there were several competitors in town, NetVision stood out significantly as the only logical choice.

A few years later, Anil entered into a partnership with some people who didn't understand the value of an outstanding client experience. Anil left the organization and the new leadership replaced the current equipment with substandard machines as they kept all the newest and most modern equipment for their own use. They replaced the high-end desks with folding tables, cancelled the daily donut order and provided photocopied certificates. They hired recently graduated students as trainers and paid them poorly. About a year later I left; a few months after that they went out of business.

Anil remains a friend and mentor to me to this day.

No matter what industry you're in, the first prerequisite to establishing your position on your Repumeter™ in preparation for your deep thought strategy is to make sure you are delivering outstanding client results and an outstanding experience.

When you do this, you could skip right over the Competitive state and directly into Branded.

PREREQUISITE #2:
Turn Them into Raving Fans

Getting outstanding results for your clients is a great (and required) start. The next step is to find a way to let the rest of the world know about it. The best way to spread the word is through raving fans.

What does "raving" mean? It means your happy clients tell their own circles of influence all about you, the results you provided and the experience you provided. And there's a simple way to make that happen: results-oriented testimonials.

Ask your happy clients to record a brief testimonial about their experience in audio or video and post it on their social media sites. In addition, you need to take those testimonials and post them on your websites, YouTube channels, wherever you have a social media presence.

Train or coach people how to speak about you by guiding their testimonial, making sure that it's results-based whenever possible. If you leave it to them to craft on their own, you run the risk of random branding.

For some examples of powerful testimonials, go to my YouTube channel (just search for Steve Lowell, you'll find me) and watch some of the testimonials I have there. You'll see that they're all results based. They include outstanding results including six-figure sales from the stage, standing ovations, higher speaking fees, more clients and other outstanding results.

Often, I'll get the objection, "No one believes testimonials, anyone can record those."

Here's my answer, try getting to Branded without them and see what happens! Good luck!

In July of 2019, Jayne and I presented a breakout session at the National Speakers Association (NSA) "Influence" convention in Denver.

After the session someone walked up to me as I was having lunch and told me he had been a member of NSA for over 20 years and my session was the best he had ever seen in his entire NSA career (an outstanding experience). How valuable would that testimonial be if I let him walk out the door without capturing that on video?

I whipped out my phone and said, "Would you mind repeating everything you just said?"

He did and it's now on my website at www.stevelowell.com/breakout

Within two weeks of that one session, we were invited to speak at several other NSA chapters across the country and by the time this book is published, we will have most likely spoken at most, if not all the NSA chapters all as a result of that one event.

Other speakers see these testimonials and want us to teach them how to achieve the same results. We do. And when they get outstanding results, we turn THEM into raving fans. Then we do it all over again.

This is all part of our deep thought strategy to pave the way for thinking bigger.

PREREQUISITE #3:
Ever-increasing Circle of Influence

Most people don't understand what their circle of influence is. It's one of those terms that has an ambiguous definition, open to interpretation.

You'll recall in the "Deciding to Become THE One," section of this book, I assigned a definition to the circle of influence for my own purposes so I could better understand its function and leverage its value.

I define my circle of influence as the population within which I can catalyze action as it relates to by business.

I chose that definition because it describes the conditions under which there's a demonstrable effect of my work (catalyzes action) where there's a potential exchange of value (they might become a client, a raving fan or an influencer).

How do you increase your circle of influence?

The best way to increase your circle of influence quickly is to find an influencer.

An influencer is a person who may or may not currently be part of your circle of influence, who is going to bring their circle of influence over and join it with yours. There are three criteria I use to qualify someone as an influencer.

First, this person must at the Branded state or above on the Repumeter™, because I want them to be influencing a lot of people. If they are in the Obscurity or Competitive states, they don't have enough influence and therefore, not enough people take action on what they do or say. When they are Branded or in the state of THE One, they have a lot more influence.

How do I know they are at the Branded state or above? It's about a gut feeling, and I go online and check their pages on social media as well as their LinkedIn profile. What I'm looking for is not their content. I'm looking for what people are saying about them. Are people talking about them in terms of results, experience and/or their expert insights? If yes, then I know they are at the Branded state or above on their own Repumeter™. It's a judgement call I make based on what others are saying about them.

Secondly, this person needs to have a large, targeted and complimentary circle of influence. Let me explain each of those.

An influencer must have a large circle of influence of their own. More than just a large circle of connection, it needs to be a circle of influence; a large population within which they can catalyze action as it relates to their business.

As an influencer, they'll need to be able to expose you and your business to lots of people and be able to encourage those people into taking some sort of action with you even if it's listening to a podcast, watching a video, attending a webinar or a live event.

In addition to being large, the influencer's circle of influence must be targeted. Their people need to need what you have.

When Sally filled the room for us in Auckland, she reached out to specific entrepreneurs and businesspeople within her large circle of influence who needed to become better speakers and monetize their expertise from the front of the room. That's a targeted audience for us.

You need to make sure that any influencers you choose to pursue have a circle of influence who needs what you do; it must be targeted.

The influencer's circle of influence must be complimentary; you must not be in competition with your influencer. In fact, your offerings should help your influencer become more valuable to their circle of influence.

You'll recall me mentioning Peggy (See "Increasing My Circle of Influence").

Over the years Peggy has been an influencer for us in part because what I do helps her become more valuable to her clients.

At the time, Peggy was helping people write their books and become bestsellers. My skills as a speaking coach helped them bring their expertise from the page to the stage and sell more books. That helps them prepare to do more work with Peggy and with me; my offerings compliment hers.

Thirdly, your influencer must be willing to advocate; they must be willing to spread the word throughout their circle of influence.

How does this happen? One of the great ways to get an influencer to advocate for you is to turn them into a raving fan. Demonstrate what you do with them; provide them outstanding results, an outstanding experience or help them benefit from your expert insights.

The reason Sally advocated for us in Auckland is because she achieved outstanding results when she worked with me. I turned her into a raving fan and, presto! An influencer.

The same thing happened with Peggy. I spoke at a few of her events, helped her prepare for some of her own speaking engagements, invited her to speak at my events at which she earned revenue — all outstanding results and/or experiences. Presto! An influencer.

There are people who can become huge influencers for you. Find them, turn them into raving fans and absorb their circle of influence into yours.

THE THREE PRIMARY MOTIVATORS

No matter your profession, if you're a financial advisor, coach, consultant or entrepreneur of any kind, getting in front of people to speak is one of the most powerful strategies you can employ to make yourself stand out and get noticed. The problem? Your competitors are catching on, and they are taking to the live stage as well, many of them speaking for free.

What does this mean for you? It means being able to deliver value through the spoken word from the front of the room is no longer a competitive advantage; it's a bare minimum requirement. You need much more than platform skill, great stories, and cool slides. Whether to an audience of one or an audience of many, you need to do more than make them think and laugh. **You need to shake their beliefs.** Let's explore how you do that.

Let's start by taking a look at why most of us do what we do.

In over 30 years of coaching speakers from around the world, I can tell you that most people who speak as part of their business are motivated by one or more of three primary motivators. These motivators form the foundation upon which we base our purpose.

For some, the motivators are powerful drivers, for others not so much. But typically, people can identify with one or more of these primary motivators.

1. A Mess

Perhaps you have what I call a mess; a huge challenge that you have overcome: an injury, an illness, abuse, an amputated limb. There is something that has shaped your world in a profound way and has made you who you are today.

I know speakers who have overcome massive challenges in their life. One was born with cerebral palsy and became an Olympic champion. Another was gang-raped by a biker gang and recovered to become a personal development expert. One lost a leg in a mountain-climbing accident. Others have survived crashes, cancer, mental illness, gender or sexual orientation prejudices and attacks.

Their motivation stems from the lessons they learned through these challenges and they feel compelled to share them with the world.

2. A Moment

Maybe you don't have a huge mess. Maybe you're more like me. I've had a pretty easy life with no major challenges to speak of. I don't have a mess. However, I do have something else. Perhaps you do too.

I have a moment; a moment in time when I realized I had a gift.

I remember a very specific event when I discovered that my gift is turning good speakers into world-class speakers. My discovery came early in my professional life.

I remember working for a very large training organization as a staff member. Speaker training was part of this company's work.

I would watch the instructors coach the speakers one at a time and I'd sit at the back coaching them in my mind. I would follow the instructors' methods very closely; sometimes admiring what I saw, sometimes disagreeing with what I saw.

One day, one of the instructors asked me if I would like to try coaching someone. I jumped at the chance!

The participant who was chosen was the toughest participant in the entire program. He didn't want to be there; his boss was forcing him. He was completely uninterested and non-participative.

Within about 30 seconds, I had him speaking passionately about what was holding him back. He came to life and never reverted back after that session.

At that moment I realized I had a gift. I was able to pull magic out of speakers they never knew was there. I was amazing at it, I loved doing it and that's when I realized I had something valuable to offer. That was my moment.

Do you have a moment in time when you realized what your purpose is? Is there a moment when you discovered your gift or your passion? Did it drive you to move forward? Maybe you have such a moment, but maybe you don't!

3. A Mission

If you don't have a mess or a moment, chances are good that you have a mission; a cause you feel driven to pursue. Perhaps there is a change in this world that you feel compelled to make; a legacy you want to leave. Your cause may be to leave some part of this world in better condition than it was when you arrived.

One of my clients in New Zealand is William. William lost a leg in a mountain climbing accident. He definitely had a mess! But more than that, William has a mission.

Because of his mess, William created The William Pike Challenge Award; "an exciting youth development program run by educators that develops young people's 21st-century skills like resilience, confidence and leadership." (Taken from his website at https://www.williampikechallenge.co.nz).

William stands as an inspiration to youth by encouraging them to become more than they ever thought they could. He provides them with challenges and recognition: this is Williams mission.

Perhaps you don't have a mess or a moment, perhaps you have a mission. Or maybe you have a little of all three.

Almost every entrepreneur I have worked with, whether they were professional speakers, coaches, financial advisors, healers, or consultants, can identify with at least one of these three motivators. Which ones do you identify with the most?

The Message

From the mess, moment or mission typically comes the message. Most messages shared by speakers are motivated by one or more of the three primary motivators.

Even non-speaking entrepreneurs can usually tie their professional messaging or the reason they do what they do back to the three primary motivators in some way.

The message may share wisdom, teach technical content, tell tales of exotic travels and/or share lessons learned along the way, and are almost always driven by the primary motivators in some way.

Entrepreneurs, especially speakers have great stories and great content sprinkled with chuckles and emotional triggers to make us laugh and cry. They have slides with jaw-dropping visuals, as well as powerful platform or sales technique, all designed to hold the audience's or prospect's attention.

Coaches, consultants and sales professionals will share their stories of how they saved a client from ruin, saved them millions of dollars or tripled their revenue. They'll have dazzling demonstrations, irrefutable statistics and jaw-dropping testimonials.

Buried within all the stories, skill and methodology is a solution to some issue – four secrets to this, five pillars of that; a new system to achieve some result. And therein lies the problem!

Every great speaker, consultant and sales professional of any kind has a solution which they share with the audience or prospect. However, when you present an amazing solution to a given problem, it makes you look and sound almost exactly the same as all the other great speakers, consultants or sales professionals of all kinds. You need to do something different; you need to think deeper. You need your expert insights.

Expert Insights:
an Overview

The term "expert insights" refers to a body of knowledge that lies deep within you, of which only you can claim ownership.

It's not your solution to any problem. It's not your unique process, three pillars, three secrets or secret matrix.

Your expert insights are an expression of your expertise, providing your audience or prospective client with a snapshot of their world from a perspective they had not previously considered. This is found by thinking much deeper about your client's condition than you have ever done before.

It's about knowing your client's world better than they do so you can help them expose the problem that causes them the most grief and then position yourself as the only logical choice, THE One!

You may be thinking to yourself "I know what that problem is!" Well, I can assure you with 99% confidence that you don't know what it is yet.

Your expert insights are a series of models, strategically designed and tactically delivered to fulfill three desired outcomes:

1. Bring your audience's or prospect's awareness to a problem they never knew they had

2. Make them present to the cost of having that problem

3. Reveal the hidden and underlying cause of the problem

Only after all three of these outcomes are fulfilled are you ready to offer a solution of any kind.

As an expert in your field, regardless of the industry or field, chances are you are far more interested in your solutions than your audience. They have been bombarded with everyone's solutions over and over again. I call it "solution fatigue."

When you speak to an audience or present to a prospect about your business, do yourself and your audiences a favor; stop peddling your solution from the platform or boardroom until and unless you have first brought to your audience's awareness a problem they never knew they had. Make them present to the cost of having that problem and THEN position yourself as the solution by demonstrating that the cause of the problem is, they don't have you.

I know this sounds like sales 101, doesn't it? Well, in a way it is, except for one thing; you'll need to go much deeper than you have gone before. Deeper than your competition and deeper than your clients have ever gone. Especially if you're preparing to go much bigger in your business. You'll need to present your audiences or prospects with a snapshot of their world they have never considered before.

When audiences and prospects see an interesting solution, they may become curious, that's not nearly enough. When you first uncover for them a problem of which they were previously unaware, they now have a need and they're much more open to hearing your solution. When we intertwine the problem and solution too early in the conversation or presentation, it sometimes comes across as a sales pitch and then you're positioning yourself to look and sound just like everyone else; you're a tennis instructor.

By applying the expert insights methodology consistently and over time, your name becomes associated with your methodology, your expert insights and not your solution. **Your reputation becomes driven by the problem you solve and not what you sell.**

You need to be able to position your expertise strategically, not primarily for the purpose of selling, but for the purpose of positioning. Making the sale is important, but it's a distant second to positioning yourself for more or bigger sales, thinking bigger.

How do you find your expert insights? That's what your deep thought strategy does.

PART FOUR

CREATING YOUR OWN DEEP THOUGHT STRATEGY

Your deep thought strategy is the process you'll use to uncover your expert insights. Your expert insights are what you present to your audiences and prospects.

Your deep thought strategy is both a research project and a creative project. The creative process will be driven by your research. The more you learn about your clients and their condition, the more creative you will be on how to find the problem they don't know they have and then present that problem to them in a way that positions you as the only logical solution.

The creative process is never linear. This means you may find yourself jumping all over the place from time to time, dropping one task to pick up another as the creative juices randomly flow from all directions at all hours of the day (and night!).

Your deep thought strategy will consume your thoughts long after you read this book and begin the work. That means you'll constantly be updating, upgrading, editing and changing the final outcome: your expert insights. All of that is okay; in fact, it's encouraged. You'll want to keep your material fresh and relevant and that often means making changes along the way, even when you're out there presenting your material to the world.

That being said, this book presents the deep thought strategy in a linear fashion, one step at a time and in sequence. But don't be frustrated if your mind jumps all over the place, especially after you have read the entire book and have a grasp on the whole picture. For this reason, **I highly recommend that you read the rest of the book before you actually do any work.** Understanding the big picture will make it so much easier because you'll have a better understanding of why things are the way they are and what leads to what.

Alrighty then, let's begin!

Packaging Your Solution

The primary purpose of your deep thought strategy is to find and craft your expert insights.

The first step in your deep thought strategy is to take a look at what you currently offer and review how you present it. We need to do this because your expert insights are going to take your audience or prospect by the hand and lead them directly to your solution, so we need to know where you will be leading them.

First, you need to answer this question: what problems do you actually solve for your clients? Make a list.

For example, if I were to do this exercise for myself it might look like this:

- They don't stand out
- They're not making the money they need to make
- They're not selling enough from the platform
- They're not closing enough sales
- They can't seem to play a bigger game
- Their audiences find them boring
- They think their own content is boring
- They know there's more for them, but they don't know how to find it

Don't be too judgmental here, list everything that comes to mind. If you're not certain what the problems are, this is your first deep thought strategy action step. Think deeper. Find out more about them and what drives them. Perhaps even call a few of your clients and ask them what problems your work has solved for them.

Second, once you have a list of the problems you solve, list the tools you use to solve them. You might use specific methodology or tools. You may have your own proprietary systems or programs; you may use solutions you buy or rent from others. It doesn't matter what the tools or systems are at this point, just list everything that comes to your mind.

For example, if I were to do this exercise for myself it might look like this:

- My Killer Keynote Template™
- The Three Circles of Speaking Energy™
- The 60-Second Miracle Sales Presentation™
- Deep Thought Strategy™

All of these are tools I have in my toolbox. These are all my own proprietary tools; yours may or may not be, it doesn't matter, we just want a list of tools that you have at your disposal to help your clients solve the problems you listed above.

Third, list the ways in which you implement those tools. You may use speaking, training, coaching, online programs, consulting or product implementation etc. List as many as you actually use.

For example, if I were to do this exercise for myself it might look like this:

- Speaking
- One-on-one mentorship
- Group coaching (Virtual)
- Live workshops
- Online training program

Once you have this prepared, it's time to package it up in a very specific way. As we go through this process, remember that you are not committing to anything yet. In fact, your entire deep thought strategy will be fluid and dynamic. Things will change multiple times before you're finished and, just when you think you're finished, it will change again as new information comes to your awareness and new ideas arise. All of that is okay.

Here's what we know so far:

We know what problems your clients are facing that you can actually help them with.

We know what tools you have at your disposal to help them with those problems.

We know the context within which you apply or deliver those tools.

The next step is to metaphorically package the entire bundle into a single package of utility, define the overall output of that utility and give that output a name.

For example, if I were to do this exercise for myself it might look like this:

1. My available tools are:
   - My Killer Keynote Template™
   - The three Circles of Speaking Energy™
   - The 60-Second Miracle Sales Presentation™
   - Deep Thought Strategy™
2. I deliver them through:
   - Speaking
   - One-on-one mentorship
   - Group coaching (Virtual)
   - Live workshops
   - Online training program
3. The output is a single, customized system they can use in their business so they can:
   - Stand out from their competitors
   - Make the money they need to make
   - Close more sales

– Sell more from the platform

– Play a bigger game

– Be more exciting to their audience

– Be more excited about their content

– Reach their highest potential

4. The name I am going to give this system they get from me is their "expert insights."

Once I complete this task, I no longer have to sell workshops, mentorship, coaching or online training programs. I no longer have to compare my content or solutions to those of my competitors to get the deal. I only have to sell one thing: expert insights.

This means if I were going through this whole process, everything I do from this point on within my deep thought strategy is to ultimately bring my audiences and prospects to expert insights.

This is my process and my output. You need to do your own. You need to find the combined output of your offerings, give that output a name and THAT'S what you sell from now on.

That means that everything YOU do from this point on within YOUR deep thought strategy is to ultimately bring YOUR audiences and prospects to "Your Solution." You'll need to name your solution.

As a point of reference and to simplify the conversation through the rest of the book, I will be referring to the solution you just identified, the output of all your offerings, as "your solution."

Take your solution and set it aside for now.

Expert Insights: A System of Models

Here's a quick review of the outcomes of the expert insights system:

1. Bring to your audience's awareness a problem they didn't know they had
2. Make them present to the cost of having that problem
3. Expose the cause of the problem

Each of these outcomes can be achieved by using models. The models might be a number of visuals that you present on a whiteboard, flip chart, slide or even on the back of a napkin. Or, they might just be represented in discussion.

If we break the expert insights system down to a series of models, there are three: the Problem Model, the Cost Model and the Cause model.

Sometimes three separate models are required, sometimes all three outcomes can be achieved with a single model. Some of my clients don't use any visual models at all; they use only their words to communicate the models. The number of models you use is not as important as reaching the three desired outcomes. If that can be done with no visual models, so be it.

When I demonstrate my Repumeter™ system (my own expert insights), I usually use three visual models.

When I'm speaking in front of an audience, I will draw the models on flip charts. I use flip charts because I like the interaction I can have with flip charts that I can't get with slides. When I use the flip charts, I can move back and forth from one to the other, I scribble on them and point to specific locations on them. They give me purposeful movement on the stage and it helps me hold the audience's attention because of all the activity. Some people find my approach to be "old school" and out of date, but I can tell you that it has been working for me all over the world with all sizes of audiences.

If I'm going to a meeting, I will usually have my Tablet with stylized pencil so I can draw the models in front of a prospect.

No matter how you express the models, you must make sure to reach all three desired outcomes. To accomplish that effectively, a tactical approach is required in the delivery of the models. Let's look at that approach next.

Problem Model

The first model in the series is what I call "The Problem Model." In this book I presented to you the Repumeter™ model, that is my problem model. At the beginning of sharing this model you may not have been aware of a problem you had, i.e. your current position on the Repumeter™.

You'll notice that the Repumeter™ Model is not a solution model. It does not share about the six pillars of success. It does not talk about the four foundational principles of leadership. It does not provide a success grid for speakers. There is nothing solution-oriented in this model. It's a problem model. The problem? You are probably thinking you're somewhere in the Obscurity or Competitive range and you want to be in the Branded or above range. Or, even if you think you're over the Branded line, you might not feel that you're quite at THE One yet. You didn't know any of that before you began reading this book.

Presenting the model alone is not enough to achieve the desired outcome of bringing to your audience's or prospect's awareness a problem they never knew they had. Certain things need to happen during the presentation of the model. You need to be able to guide your audience or prospect a certain way. Let me explain.

As I presented the Repumeter™, never did I suggest where you are on the scale How would I know that? I had to explain the model in such a way that you self-identified with your rank on the model. I did that by virtue of the definition of each of the four states.

This is where some deep thought comes in.

When designing my problem model, in this case the Repumeter™, I needed to first know my audience (presumably in this case, that's you) so well that I could present you with a snapshot of your condition in a manner in which you can recognize your own location.

I did that by establishing four states or stages, all of which define a different condition. As I defined these conditions, you were looking for where you fit on the scale; the condition(s) that best described your reality.

As I listed the names of each state (Obscurity, Competitive, Branded and THE One), I also gave you multiple opportunities to self-identify with one or more of these states.

I provided a single-sentence definition of each:

Obscurity: people in your circles don't really know who you are or what you do.

Competitive: people in your circles have a pretty good idea of what you do, but there's nothing that separates you from everybody else who does what you do.

Branded: people in your circles know who you are and what you do, and there is beginning to be something noticeable about you, but they may not be able to define exactly what that is.

THE One: You are no longer in a category of many, you are no longer in a category of a few; you are now a category of one, the only logical choice.

Those single-sentence definitions gave you a general idea of the nature of the condition. Some (maybe most) readers and audience members are able to begin self-identifying just by the definition alone.

For each state, after naming it and defining it, I "populated" it with the recognizable symptoms that you would observe if you were in that stage. For each state I said "You know you're in this state when..." followed by a list of symptoms.

It's the list of symptoms at each state that finalizes the self-selection process for you. As you read (or listened to) the list of symptoms, you're checking them off in your mind one at a time. At some point you'll check off enough symptoms that you'll associate with one or more of the proposed states.

When I designed the states on the Repumeter™, I designed them according to clusters of recognizable symptoms and tactically present them so that almost everyone is in a state other than THE One. Most people find themselves somewhere between Obscurity and Competitive, a few find themselves at Branded and the odd person identifies with THE One.

The point is, unless you honestly identified with THE One, you're in the wrong spot! That's the problem you never knew you had.

Previously I asked you if you knew where you were on The Repumeter™. In your head you said "yes" or "no." Then I asked you if you were exactly where you want or need to be. Do you remember your answers?

I always ask my audiences this question, whether there are hundreds or thousands of people, by saying, "Put up your hand if you know where you are on this model of the Repumeter™," and every hand in the place goes up because they can pinpoint their location.

After all the hands go up, I say, "Keep your hand up if you are exactly where you want to be." And every hand goes down, which means everybody in the audience is in the wrong spot. **That's the point of the problem model; they need to self-identify in an undesirable state.** Once they self-identify as being in the undesirable state, you have just brought to their attention a problem they didn't know they had.

In many cases, this one outcome alone is enough to generate legitimate and intense interest in you and your solutions. But it's still too early to start selling yet.

HOW TO CRAFT
YOUR PROBLEM MODEL

I mentioned earlier that crafting your expert insights system is not a linear process; you may have to bounce back and forth and edit different parts of your system as you discover new information and as new ideas are revealed through the creative process.

There are three questions, the answers to which form the foundation of your problem model. It's the answering of these questions that requires most of the deep thought. And it's between these answers where you are most likely to wander back and forth from one to the next. As the answer to one becomes clear, that of another may become more uncertain.

1. Who is the audience to which my solution applies?

2. What is their condition for which my solution provides utility?

3. From what perspective does their condition require my solution?

Let's explore how to answer each of these questions.

1. Who is the audience to which my solution applies?

"Who's your audience?" is the first question asked by every business, marketing or speaker coach. The most common response is to list those who use our products or services. If I were to ask a business coach this question, she might say "entrepreneurs" or "small business owners." If I were to ask a sales professional, he might respond with "technology companies" or "large corporations." Ask a human resources consultant and she might say "the HR department." Though any of these could be correct; for the purposes of crafting a problem model, they may not be complete.

Remembering that the purpose of the problem model is to bring to their awareness a problem they never knew they had, we first need to know who "they" are. In addition, as you execute the deep thought strategy to find the problem they never knew they had, you may find the symptoms of the problem are found within an adjacent population, in which case defining the audience may not be as straightforward.

Begin with the economic buyer; who actually makes the buying decision? Sometimes it's the actual user of your products or services, sometimes it's not.

To demonstrate, let's look at two different situations, one in which defining the audience is simple; the other in which defining the audience is much more complex: Barry the executive presentations coach and Jill the corporate purchasing consultant.

For Barry the executive presentations coach, defining the audience might be quite simple; he works directly with executives to change an outcome and improve the executive's condition in some way. Chances are good that it's the executive herself who uses the service and who also makes the buying decision.

In this case, the symptoms of the problem would most likely be observable directly within the executives' condition; she doesn't get the results she needs from her presentations because of her lack of skill. Barry changes the skill level thus changing the condition, pretty straightforward.

For Jill the corporate purchasing consultant, defining the audience is likely more complex.

Jill helps corporations improve their purchasing function to reduce costs and increase margins.

Let's assume for Jill, the economic buyer is the Chief Financial Officer (CFO) and Jill does her work directly with the purchasing staff.

Jill's economic buyer is the CFO, but the one who influences the CFO to make the buying decision might be one of the directors. The problem that the director doesn't know he has may manifest itself at the bottom line, but also with the staff, an adjacent population.

Through your deep thought strategy, you may find there are multiple audiences engaged in your problem model:

1. The economic buyer
2. The buying influencer
3. The end user

The audience to whom you should target your problem model is the buying influencer. It's the buying influencer's condition that your solution needs to change, and the symptoms of that condition may be found at the end user level.

For your deep thought strategy to reveal the right problem model, you'll need to know the journey of both your buying influencer and your end user. You may be solving your buying influencer's problem by implementing your solution with the end user, and they may not be the same population.

Take the time to explore your audience and their condition. It may happen that you'll get well into defining your problem model and you'll find that you need to redefine your audience.

2. What is the condition for which my solution provides utility?

Now that we've established your problem model should be targeted to your buying influencer, we can begin exploring the condition around which your problem model will be crafted, the audience's journey.

You need to be creative here. You will be representing a version of the typical client condition as it relates to your audience, but you need to do it from a perspective different than what the prospect expects, making it unique to you. This helps to position you as THE One in your prospect's mind. How do you do that? Read on.

Consider the problems your solution (which you have already defined) actually solves. Ask yourself how those problems show up in the every-day life of your clients. What do they see, think and feel as a result of having those problems in their lives? These are the symptoms that your clients, audiences and prospects will recognize. List as many as you can.

Cluster those symptoms into states or stages that define the prospect's condition according to your observations based on the clusters, and now you have the beginning of your problem model. Simple right?

Let's use Jill the corporate purchasing consultant as a hypothetical example.

Jill's buying influencer is the Procurement Director. Jill's task is to bring the Director's awareness to a problem he never knew he had. To start with, Jill needs to demonstrate that she knows the Director's world as well as he does. She'll do that by clustering recognizable symptoms into states or stages that allow the Director to self-select into one or more of those states or stages.

Jill will present four stages that companies find themselves in, concerning procurement:

At stage one the company almost always pays full price for materials and the quality of service provided by their suppliers is poor. Their cost of goods is always over budget, their margins are often below projections and the bottom line is suffering. Purchasing staff is hard to retain; they often stay a short time and then leave the company.

At stage two the company pays the same for materials over a long period of time. Negotiations are done through tender and are time consuming and often don't result in much savings. The service offered by suppliers is tolerable but not great. As a result, there is little or no effort to negotiate better contracts with suppliers. To reduce the cost of goods, the company uses other creative means. Staff are committed but often seem overworked and stressed.

At stage three, materials procurement is smooth, and the service offered by suppliers is acceptable. The purchasing staff can negotiate the odd deal, but they work hard at it. Margins are as projected but it's hard to find creative ways to improve profitability. Purchasing staff stay until they have a strong skillset and then often leave for a higher-paying or more senior position with one of your competitors.

At stage four, suppliers pursue you by consistently offering incentives. They provide exceptional service; they are easy to negotiate with and seem to give the order from your company priority status. Your margins are strong and are well-reflected in the bottom line. Purchasing staff are career employees, do their jobs well and enjoy their work.

Jill would have defined these four states based on clusters of observable symptoms. The prospect can self-identify with one or more of the four states. Jill already knows the vast majority of her prospective clients will self-select in states one or two because she will target her efforts at pursuing those prospects and they will recognize the symptoms in those states.

With this, Jill has made clear a problem that is recognizable to the prospect, but it's not yet a problem the prospect never knew he had. The prospect will recognize those symptoms but there's nothing here yet that offers them a new perspective they have never considered before. Jill needs to go to the next step in crafting the problem model, defining the perspective from which her solution becomes relevant.

Jill's prospect will recognize the symptoms within the states she describes and applies to his company. At the same time, he'll be thinking of all the solutions he has tried in the past to solve the problem he recognizes, and he'll be justifying some of those problems as being normal or unsolvable. It's possible that he might be actively looking for a solution.

No matter what the prospect is thinking at this time, chances are superb that none of his thoughts are going to be in Jill's favor as a potential solution. All Jill has done to this point is have him acknowledge that there is a known problem.

Jill needs to show the problem to the prospect through a different lens. She needs to position the problem from a perspective the prospect has not considered before.

Other consultants will try to convince this prospect that he needs to make internal changes. He needs to improve his purchasing function, refine his negotiating strategy, strengthen his onboarding and training programs for new recruits and improve the work environment.

Jill's solution may offer all those things, but if she presents them at this point and in this way, she is making herself look and sound like every other consultant. She would be locking herself into the state of Competitive. What does she need to do? She needs to change the context, change the perspective.

3. From what perspective does the prospect's condition require my solution?

To change the perspective Jill will take the states she has created which contain observable symptoms and redirect the source of which they are a reflection. She will not define these states as a collective reflection of what's happening inside the company, which the prospect already knows. She will define these states as a collective reflection of what's happening outside the company. Jill will define these states as a collective reflection of how suppliers view the company as a client, and attribute all the observable symptoms to that, and not to the internal improvements that need to be made.

What follows is a hypothetical example of how Jill might present her problem model from an alternative perspective:

In my 20 years working with procurement and purchasing teams, I have found that a company's ability to attract top suppliers, negotiate the best contracts and secure the best service is not just established by volume; it's directly related to a predetermined mindset with which potential suppliers view the company.

There are four states in which potential suppliers view any prospective client.

The first state is what I call "Adverse." Adverse means suppliers see your business as being a burden they'll need to tolerate.

You know your company is in this state when you almost always pay full price for materials and the quality of service provided by your suppliers is poor. Your cost of goods is always over budget, your margins are too low, and the bottom line is suffering. Your purchasing staff is hard to retain; they often stay a short time and then leave the company.

The second state is what I call "Endurable." Endurable means your suppliers see you as an easy client who requires little servicing to maintain.

You know your company is in this state when your company pays the same for materials over a long period of time. Negotiations are done through tender and are time-consuming and often don't result in much savings. The service offered by suppliers is tolerable but not great. As a result, there is little or no effort to negotiate better contracts with suppliers. To reduce the cost of goods your company uses other creative means. Staff are committed but often seem overworked and stressed.

The third state is what I call "Favored." Favored means suppliers see you as a client they want to keep and are willing to offer some concessions to keep you.

You know your company is in this state when materials procurement is smooth, and the service offered by suppliers is acceptable. Your purchasing staff can negotiate the odd deal, but they work hard at it. Margins are as projected but it's hard to find creative ways to improve profitability. Purchasing staff stay until they have a strong skillset and then often leave for a higher-paying or more senior position with one of your competitors.

The fourth stage is what I call "Preferred." Preferred means that your suppliers consider it a badge of honor to be your supplier and they are willing to work for your business.

You know your company is in this state when suppliers pursue you by consistently offering incentives. They provide exceptional service; they are easy to negotiate with and seem to give orders from your company priority status. Your margins are strong and are well-reflected in the bottom line. Purchasing staff are career employees, do their jobs well and enjoy their work.

Even though Jill changed the perspective from an internal issue to an external issue, notice how the recognizable symptoms are the same. Now the prospect sees the symptoms as a reflection of his company's reputation in addition to internal deficiencies.

Jill's prospect has just become aware of a problem he never knew he had; his suppliers see his company as someone they have to endure, not pursue.

By bringing her prospect's awareness to a problem he never knew he had, Jill has positioned herself as someone with unique knowledge of her prospect's world.

Of course, in reality Jill would have to secure proof of concept by having some of her supplier contacts and existing or past clients validate the veracity of her model. She would likely have to make changes to her information to more accurately reflect the reality of the procurement world. But once that validation is done, she could present this model to actual prospects and most likely stand out as a result.

Ignite Aspiration

Your problem model should be tactically designed to ignite aspiration within your prospect or audience. It should give them something to aspire to. There are two components to igniting aspiration from the problem model:

1. Calculated state or stage positioning

2. Critical point positioning

Calculated state or stage positioning is achieved when your states or stages are defined in such a way that your prospects not only self-select their own position within those states or stages, but the state or stages in which they self-select are undesirable states.

Your problem model should contain four states or stages (five states maximum). In a four-state model, the first two states should be undesirable and include the symptoms with which most of your prospects will identify. You want your prospects and audiences to self-select into one of the two undesirable states.

The third state is a semi-desirable state. It's a state to which a few will self-select. Those who fall into the first two states will aspire to be in this third state. It's an attainable goal which entices them into making some small forward steps in their mind.

The last state should be almost unattainable. This is the state where your prospects and audience would love to be, but maybe can't clearly see themselves ever getting there.

Critical Point Positioning will happen at the third state. This is the semi-desirable state to which most of your audience will aspire. There are three properties which make this state a critical point:

1. It's a tipping point at which the states move from undesirable to desirable provided certain conditions are met. This tipping point is a critical line on your problem model that absolutely must be crossed in order to move to the desirable state. On the Repumeter™ the Branded state is the tipping point. It's the re-association of your name that changes and brings you across that critical line at Branded and towards THE One.

2. It's a tentative state. If the tipping point conditions are not met, they slide back into the undesirable states.

3. This is the point at which your solution begins to become relevant. Your solution is what allows them to meet the tipping point conditions and proceed towards the desirable state.

The end result is your prospect or audience finds themselves in an undesirable state with a better state within reasonable reach at a critical tipping point that needs to be crossed to make it into the most desirable state. And they'll see all this from a perspective they had never considered before.

When you present your problem model in this manner, you not only create desire within your prospect or audience to improve their condition, but you have begun the process of positioning yourself as the only logical choice to help them do that.

AVOIDING DISQUALIFIERS

To ensure your problem model reaches the desired outcome, it's critical that your prospect or audience is able to self-select their own position. If you tell them where they are on your problem model, you have defeated the purpose of the process. Similarly, disqualifiers are symptoms or states that cause your prospect to immediately disassociate, defeating the purpose of the process.

Your prospects and audiences will evaluate the states on your problem model by the symptoms that define them, and then self-select into one or more of your states. This happens because they will evaluate the symptoms according to three criteria:

1. This does happen to me

2. This does not happen to me

3. This is not who I am

A symptom is a disqualifier if it meets the third criterion.

An example of a disqualifying symptom might be one that defines a demographic. For example, "You know you're in this state if you are a young entrepreneur and you're not getting taken seriously by your prospects."

It's possible that your prospect may relate to all the other symptoms in the state or stage, but not associate with the demographic. One could be 50 years old and still not be taken seriously by his prospects. When this prospect evaluates this symptom, he could disqualify himself from the state because he's not a young entrepreneur, that's not him.

A symptom that includes tenure would also be a possible disqualifier: "You know you're in this state when you have been in business for 10 years and you still struggle with revenue."

Your prospect may associate with the symptom of struggling with revenue but be new in business. This could cause your prospect to disassociate from that state because she has not been in business for 10 years.

In my experience, a prospect may associate with four out of six qualifying symptoms and still self-identify with that state as a result. But if there's one disqualifier based on demographics or tenure, they can associate with all of the qualifying symptoms, but not self-select the state because of one disqualifier.

Demographics and tenure are not the only possible disqualifiers. When you craft your problem model, you need to ensure that you are not including any disqualifiers that meet the third criterion.

The name of your state could also be a disqualifier.

When naming the states or stages on your problem model, be sure the name labels the condition of the state and not the people in it.

To make it easy for your prospect or audience to self-select, they need to be able to do so without adopting a personal label. For example, the first state on my Repumeter™ is "Obscurity" not "Obscure."

A prospect can self-identify with a state, but not personally adopt the label. He can accept that his condition is one of obscurity but may not be able to accept the he himself is obscure. If the name of the state was "Obscure," it would be much more difficult for a prospect to self-select because they would be adopting a personal and undesirable label.

This applies specifically with the undesirable states. When labeling the most desirable state, it can be advantageous to apply a more personal label because your prospect may be enticed by the label.

On my Repumeter™ the ultimate state is called "THE One;" who wouldn't want to bear that label?

Choosing a
Shape for Your Problem Model

Your problem model can be presented in any form. I use an arc, some use a triangle, a flow chart, a house; there is no specific shape that works best. However, there are some things to consider when selecting the best shape for your problem model. Here are a few:

1. Is the model a series of static states in which your prospect usually finds themselves to the exclusion of the other states? If so, some image that represents specific points might be best.

2. Is the model a series of stages that your prospects navigate through on the way to a destination? In this case a process flow shape might serve you.

3. Does the model present a series of hierarchical levels? Possibly an organizational chart might work here.

4. Does the model represent a cycle in which the prospect gets caught up? Perhaps a circular flow with arrows might work well here.

Once you know your states and stages, and your critical point, ask yourself what it might look like. Go to the internet and search for keywords and images that come from your model, and see if you can find a visual that you might adopt and apply to your model.

Not all models need a visual representation, but I have found that presenting your problem model visually helps your prospect or audience self-select.

As you craft your problem model, review this section often and make sure your problem model conforms to all the criteria we have covered to the highest degree possible. Remember, your objective with your problem model is to bring to their awareness a problem they never knew they had.

The Cost Model

The second model in the series is "The Cost Model." The focus of this model is to draw attention to the cost of having the problem they never knew they had.

To accomplish this, you need to know the currency of your audience or prospect. Not all audiences are driven by money in every situation; there are other currencies that become important: freedom, influence, time, etc.

Once you've identified the currencies that motivate your audience the most, you can demonstrate the costs associated with each state on the problem model.

For example, when my audiences use my Repumeter™ model, to identify the specific state of their reputation, I compare that state against the three currencies that speakers and coaches value most: influence, impact and income.

Once I demonstrate that being in "Obscurity" or "Competitive" on their Repumeter™ costs them dearly in influence and, by extension, impact and income, they become more motivated to do what needs to be done to move past those states and into "Branded" and "THE One."

You need to know what currencies your audience or prospects value most. Show a correlation between the states on your problem model and the costs associated with each state using the relevant currencies.

I usually present my cost model on a basic coordinate grid. I show high and low influence, impact and income on the "Y" axis (vertical axis on the left) and I position the four Repumeter™states on the "X" axis (along the bottom). I show how operating in Obscurity and Competitive result in very low influence, impact and income and how operating at THE One results in the highest level of influence, impact and income. This gives my audience a visual representation of what it's costing them to be in the wrong state.

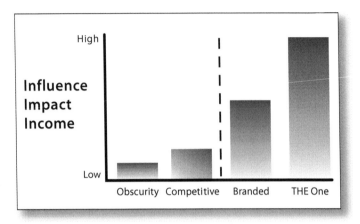

It's important that your claims be true. Your audience or prospect must be able to nod their head in agreement with what you are demonstrating. That's why I call this entire process the deep thought strategy. You need to think deeply enough to ensure that you know your audience's world so well that you are hitting all the right buttons with your problem model and your cost model. If your models and explanation do not cause them to nod their head, figuratively or otherwise, your models are not hitting the mark and you need to go even deeper.

Once they see that being in the wrong state is at a significant cost, they become a little more motivated to explore your solution (hold on, you're still not ready for that just yet).

THE CAUSE MODEL

The third model in the series is "The Cause Model." This is where you expose the cause of the problem and position yourself as the only logical solution.

The key in presenting the cause model is being able to demonstrate that the cause of the problem is they are not using your solution. You must be able to demonstrate it without them knowing what your solution is beyond its name. They need no details yet.

For example, when I present my Repumeter™ model, and then show the cost model associated with it, I then demonstrate the cause by sharing the three primary motivators (mess, moment or mission) and how most speakers and entrepreneurs craft their message based on their solutions derived from those motivators. Up to that point most people will agree, and they will self-identify with what I am presenting. But then I throw a curve ball. I say, "that's the problem!"

I go on to explain the reason they are on the wrong spot on the Repumeter™ is because they are doing what everyone else does; they base their messaging on their solutions. What they need to do to get to THE One on their Repumeter™ is base their message on their expert insights (the name of my solution).

The question arises; what the heck are these expert insights? Well, that's what I do; I help you craft your own expert insights using what I call a deep thought strategy so you can position yourself as THE One on your Repumeter™ and prepare yourself to start thinking bigger.

Can you see how all this comes together?

By demonstrating the cause of their problem, that they are not creating and applying their own expert insights when they speak or present, I've helped them recognize the need for them to do that. Everyone wants to learn how to do that, then they can solve the problem they didn't know they had.

EXPERT INSIGHTS IN ACTION

To help you get clarity on the concept of expert insights and how they apply in differed environments, I have provided some case studies from a diverse selection of professions. In each case study I briefly explain the problem model used, the problem that's exposed and the solution that's being positioned.

Expert Insights in Action Case Study

Grant: Team Decision Making

In early 2019, Jayne and I attended the Asian Professional Speakers of Singapore convention in Singapore.

I presented the Repumeter™ and introduced the concept of expert insights. I gave no instructions on how to discover, craft or present expert insights (there wasn't enough time). I gave the audience no more information than you have now about the concept.

Afterwards we were inundated with requests to find out more. This happens every time I present this content.

One of those individuals requesting more information was Grant.

Grant is well known for his adventures as an explorer. He navigates dangerous parts of the world over land and sea using only human-powered devices, most of which he manufactures himself. He has summited Mount Everest, crossed some of the world's most dangerous waters and has endured mental, emotional and physical challenges few have experienced.

As a result of his adventures, Grant has become an expert in decision-making in volatile and unstable environments where the consequences of failure are high (often life-threatening). He wanted to bring his decision-making process to the corporate world as a speaker and a trainer. He was doing both well but wanted to think bigger.

For Grant, thinking bigger meant getting more well known, but he found himself competing with other experts who had different offerings, but who were contenders for the same business. He would find himself explaining why his solution was better than their solution and it became more and more competitive.

When Grant saw the Repumeter™, he realized he had a problem he never knew he had; he was in the wrong spot on the Repumeter™. He knew it was costing him business and reputation and he needed expert insights, whatever expert insights means! He joined us.

Grant knew that his corporate clients all want basically the same things. They want a stronger bottom line, better productivity, and they want their teams and departments to work better together. What company doesn't want those things?

Every prospect presents Grant with a problem that needs to be solved. This is where Grant (and pretty much everyone else) would get sucked into the competitive state by offering a solution to the problem the prospect identifies.

It makes sense, doesn't it? The prospect expresses a problem; the expert offers a solution and a deal is made, right? Wrong!

Here's how it really works: the prospect expresses a problem; the expert offers a solution and the prospect looks at other options. Now the expert is in competition with other experts. Grant is competing against price, value proposition, credibility, reputation and everything else that the competitive environment consists of.

Grant needed to change the language he uses to appear to be different from his competitors. His unique solutions alone wouldn't do that. He needed his own expert insights. To accomplish that, he needed to execute a deep thought strategy.

When Grant meets with a prospect or speaks at an event, his immediate job is not to solve the problem the prospect identifies.

Grant's job is to demonstrate that what the prospect has identified as the problem is really just a symptom. Grant has to bring the prospect's awareness to the actual problem that's causing the symptom; the problem they never knew they had.

Typically, Grant would tell his prospect about his simulations (which happen to be extremely cool, by the way!) within which he has high-end videos from his expeditions of dangerous situations in which decisions must be made. He uses those videos as part of an interactive training program around effective decision-making. Sounds amazing, doesn't it?

But his prospects aren't buying simulations, they're buying a solution to a problem, so they want to see what else is out there. We had to get Grant away from selling his solution and on to selling a problem the prospect never knew they had; a problem that not only makes Grant's simulations a targeted solution, a problem that makes Grant's simulations the ONLY solution.

Over the next four months or so he and I implemented a deep thought strategy; we explored his expertise at the forensic level to identify three things:

1. What EXACTLY is the problem Grant's clients have that they never knew they had?
2. What was that problem costing them?
3. What was causing that problem?

After a few months of very intense discussions, we determined that organizations fall into specific patterns around important team decision-making. These patterns are recognizable to Grant as the expert, but not to the prospect.

Grant demonstrates within every organization there are four decision-making states, each one appropriate for specific decision environments. These are states that Grant has defined from his own experience and expertise. He can now show where almost every organization applies the wrong decision-making state to the wrong decision environment. Further, Grant shows how each organization has a decision-making culture based on one of the four decision-making states, and how that culture almost always results in an ineffective decision-making process in situations where the consequences of failure are high.

When Grant demonstrates this, his prospects see a snapshot of their world they have never considered before. They become aware of a problem they never knew they had; they have the wrong decision-making culture based on the wrong state, something they would never have come up with themselves.

He demonstrates these things by using visual models, each model created by Grant, each has a name Grant has assigned.

Grant then shows them the cause of the problem is they need, what Grant calls a "Decision-Making Culture Shift" (Grant's solution). The "Decision-Making Culture Shift" includes defining, implementing and activating three "Decision Alignment Drivers," another term Grant's clients can attach his name to.

Guess what Grant's simulations provide? They help companies implement their own "Decision-Making Culture Shift" by helping them define, implement and activate their decision alignment drivers (as well as other things).

With this process, Grant disqualifies his competition because he becomes the only logical choice.

The decision-making states, decision environments, decision-making culture, decision-making culture shift, decision alignment drivers and all of Grant's simulations combine to become Grant's expert insights. His name now becomes associated with his models for identifying decision-making inadequacies, not just his simulations. Grant found all of that by applying a deep thought strategy.

In his globally expanding circles, Grant is THE One for corporate team decision-making speaking and training. Now he's ready to think big, and he is!

Within a month or so of finalizing his expert insights, Grant presented them to a Facebook executive who then hired him to speak at the launch of their newest headquarters in Singapore. No doubt a launching pad into much bigger things for Grant!

Greg: Moments that Matter

Greg is an award-winning Master of Ceremonies from New Zealand. His reputation as a Master of Ceremonies positions him as THE One on his Repumeter™ within his substantial circles in New Zealand, Australia and several other countries.

Greg wanted to make a lateral move and add keynote speaking to his activities; he wanted to think bigger. But his problem was his reputation as an emcee was standing in the way. He was known as an emcee, not a speaker. How was he going to go bigger and add keynote speaking to his reputation? As an emcee he's THE One, as a speaker he's barely above Obscurity.

Greg had lots of passion and experience and felt he wanted to bring to the world a motivational message. But the world is full of motivational messages and for him to stand out he needed something different. He needed to bring his audiences a problem they never knew they had. He needed to think deeper; he needed his own expert insights and for that he needed to execute his own deep thought strategy.

Other motivational speakers will offer their unique solution: their four pillars to success, the five secrets to happiness, the new law of attraction enhancer, a better NLP course or some other solution.

Of course, Greg has a solution to offer, but speaking about his solution would simply immerse him into a category of many and he would fall prey to the think big illusion.

Greg and I worked together for several months, often several hours at a time. We excavated as many stories and ideas as we could find, discarded 95% of them and found some common themes with which we could work.

The primary theme Greg wanted to present was called "Moments that Matter." But there are so many speakers who talk about similar concepts in one way or another, we had to find a way for Greg to present a different perspective, a snapshot of his audience's world from a perspective they had never considered before; a problem they never knew they had.

We tried and tested hundreds of ideas and concepts, and we arrived at five stages of awareness that people experience. Of the five stages, only one prepares you for recognizing "Moments that Matter" and then seizing the opportunity presented by each of these moments.

When Greg speaks about this now, he first acknowledges the symptoms that people see in their lives and recognize as problems; they're not happy, healthy or fulfilled in some way. They're not as prosperous as they would like to be, their relationships are not as strong as they would like them to be or they just don't feel they have reached their potential in some way. Pretty common stuff, right? You can see how Greg, as another motivational speaker with another solution could get swallowed up unless he has something new. Greg has something new; his expert insights.

When Greg speaks, through his own stories and experiences, he acknowledges a wide range of symptoms that everyone in his audience can relate to. Through those symptoms he reveals his five stages of awareness. He shows how being anywhere other than the fifth stage will prevent them from recognizing and leveraging the opportunities associated with "Moments that Matter."

What's the problem they never knew they had? They're in the wrong stage of awareness. How do they get into the right stage? They need Greg!

Greg now has his own expert insights; something unique with which his name can be associated. Greg used a deep thought strategy to find those expert insights. He had to think deeper about what his audiences experience in their lives, what they think and what they feel. This took Greg and I several months to assemble.

From that research and introspection, we clustered the symptoms into Greg's five stages of awareness. We named and defined each stage, determined what keeps people stuck in each stage and we found a way to position Greg as the only logical solution to get them unstuck.

The next step was to work towards getting his name associated with his model that reveals his states of awareness.

Did Greg's deep thought strategy work for him? Well, he's now an award-winning, international keynote speaker.

Valerie: Mental Health Professional

Valerie is a trained and experienced mental health professional. She's also a former mental health patient. She suffered with Post Traumatic Stress Disorder (PTSD) and hoarding.

Valerie's expertise is helping those who suffer with PTSD and hoarding to overcome their condition to the point where they can live a more normal and healthy life. She did have clients who paid her for this service, but she found it difficult to build a sustainable business from within the client base itself. Valerie had to find a way to generate business through referrals from others in the mental health field.

Mental health professionals are not quick to refer outside help. Valerie needed a way to position herself as a reliable resource they could refer their patients to with confidence.

Valerie created a model in the shape of a house. Inside the house represented the stages of the illness's progression and what the patient actually experiences at home; something most mental health professionals don't get to witness. This became the problem the mental health professionals didn't know they had, the hidden experiences of their patients at home.

Because Valerie experienced living as the person inside the house, she brings knowledge and a perspective which most mental health professionals don't get the opportunity to witness or learn about. And because she's also a mental health professional, she has the credentials and the credibility to support her assertions.

On the outside of the house she positioned the various mental health professionals: social workers on one side of the house, psychologists and psychotherapists on the other side, psychiatrists along the top.

When she presents the model to mental health professionals, social workers, psychologists, psychotherapists and psychiatrists, she demonstrates their respective roles and shows how her work with the patient inside the house helps support the work each of them offers the patient from the outside.

She demonstrates that her direct influence inside the home with the patient helps them implement the work offered by the other mental health professionals. This makes it far more likely that the patient returns to a normal and healthy lifestyle.

Before presenting her model to her peers or the public, Valerie tested it with several of her colleagues in the mental health profession. She made some minor adjustments based on their input until she was able to validate through her peers that her model was accurate and correct.

To validate the integrity of her model from those who live inside the house, Valerie presented her model to some live groups of non-mental health professionals, including some who would be considered patients and care givers.

Valerie is now a regular speaker at national and international mental health conferences and conventions because of her model, her expert insights.

It was her deep thought strategy that allowed her to develop her expert insights and position herself as THE One in her field, the only logical choice.

Diana: Marketing & Business Coach

Diana, a marketing and business coach is in a very crowded space in the market. There are many coaches like Diana who do many of the same things.

Diana understood that she was in an uber-crowded field. She had 30 years of entrepreneurial experience. Her credentials were similar to many others with whom she competes.

She became an Amazon best-selling author which gave her instant credibility with a much wider audience. Her book became a "glorified business card" she could use as an introduction to potential clients, but all that wasn't enough to put her out front and make her the marketing coach of choice.

Diana developed her expert insights and formulated a model for her clients that demonstrates the various levels at which business owners must operate. The levels she demonstrates are defined by the activities that consume their time. Her model shows a correlation between the dominant business activities and the success of the business. The problem that's revealed for most of her audience is they operate within their business at a level that is not congruent with where they want their business to be; they are operating at the wrong level.

Her solution is called "The Entrepreneur's Distinct Natural Advantage (DNA)" which positions her as the only logical choice to help them correct their operating position and bring their business to where they want it to be.

She started using her models while closing sales with prospects over the phone. In addition, she took her models to the platform where she began presenting them to larger audiences.

Diana used her expert insights system for a while and saw a marked increase in business. She admits that she set the models aside for a while and during that time she saw a drop in her business. Once she reinstated the models into her content and started using her expert insights again, business increased again, and she has seen a significant increase since.

Yvonne: Resilience Expert

Yvonne is a Licensed Professional Counselor, a Licensed Substance Abuse Treatment Practitioner, and a Clinically Certified Domestic Violence Counselor.

She's also a speaker who has extraordinary stories of resilience to share based on her own trials and challenges including surviving cancer, the death of her only child, an abusive relationship and a very difficult and messy divorce.

Yvonne's theme is "Moving from Broken to Beautiful." She's written a series of books based on this theme. It's a very nice theme, but it's been used many times by many different people in one form or another. That doesn't make the theme unusable for Yvonne, it just doesn't make her stand out.

In addition, Yvonne is a woman of very strong faith. She is accustomed to bringing her faith into her presentations. As she began thinking bigger to include the general market, she dropped the spiritual references. However, she has a profound message to share for which she gives God the credit.

Yvonne speaks to help people who struggle with moving from broken to beautiful after experiencing life-altering tragedy. It's a noble and beautiful mission. But it's a space in which she could easily get lost in a sea of sameness; she would be at the Obscurity stage on the Repumeter™.

Yvonne wanted to think bigger and bring her message to the world but thinking bigger was not getting her noticed. She needed a deep thought strategy; she needed her own expert insights.

For almost a year Yvonne and I explored her stories, experiences and wisdom. What finally emerged were Yvonne's five "Challenge Response" stages. Three of those stages fall below "The Decision Line." To navigate the "Challenge Response" stages and rise above "The Decision Line" into the final stage (where everyone wants to be), one needs to strengthen their "Purpose Profile."

All this content is unique to Yvonne. Sure, some of the words have been used before, even the term "Purpose Profile" has been used, but not in the context within which Yvonne applies it. The combination of Yvonne's model and her rendition of "The Purpose Profile" is unique to her; that combination comprises her expert insights.

By presenting her "Challenge Response" stages and the "Decision Line," Yvonne brings to her audience's awareness a problem they never knew they had; they're living below "The Decision Line." If they want to move forward with their lives, they need to get above "The Decision Line," and to do that they need Yvonne's help with their "Purpose Profile."

Now Yvonne has a unique message. She can add as much or as little of her faith as she likes according to the audience to which she's speaking, and her name is becoming associated with her "Purpose Profile" model.

And, by the way, Yvonne has also since become an award-winning, international speaker!

Thinking bigger was of no value to Yvonne until she began thinking deeper. Through her deep thought strategy, she arrived at her expert insights and now she's successfully thinking bigger.

Laura: Human Resources Lawyer

Laura owns a multi award-winning Human Resources (HR) law firm, and an HR consulting firm just outside of Toronto. She's also a dynamic and sought-after speaker in the Canadian HR world.

Demand for Laura's services was growing. She estimates she was near the Branded state on her own Repumeter™ when she met me, but she wanted to be THE One. She needed a keynote message that would take her beyond the usual legal talk most lawyers present; she wanted something that was uniquely hers.

Laura and I worked together from June 2018 until June 2019 crafting some of her messaging. A large part of that work was a deep thought strategy to find Laura's expert insights.

Laura and I would meet for a half day every six weeks or so and work intensively, diving deep into her expertise and into the minds of her clients from an HR perspective. What we uncovered was a series of states in which businesses can find themselves as defined by their knowledge of, and attitude towards HR law.

Laura describes the states according to observable behaviors and known attitudes within any organization. She plots the states on a grid which associates each state with level of risk exposure and potential costs that could result from an HR incident, human rights complaint or a harassment claim. On the same grid she shows the cost of implementing proper HR policies and creating an organizational culture that supports a strong HR philosophy.

By the time she's done presenting, her audience can easily identify what state they're in (the problem they never knew that had), the risk exposure associated with their state (the cost in a relevant currency) and how NOT having proper HR policies is far more expensive than investing in them (the cause of the problem).

When Laura enlightens her audience with her stages and related comparisons (her expert insights), she automatically positions herself as THE One; she becomes the only logical choice. Now she has content that no other HR lawyer has.

Summarizing Your Deep Thought Strategy

Thinking big is not likely to result in anything good unless you first think deep. That's what your deep thought strategy does.

The purpose of your deep thought strategy is to find your expert insights.

The term "expert insights" refers to a perspective that comes from deep within your experience and of which only you can claim ownership.

To find your expert insights you need to think far deeper than you have to date. You need to know your clients' world better than they do, doing that work is your deep thought strategy.

Start by packing your solution into a single entity and giving it a name. The solution I offer is called "expert insights." You'll need to package your solution into a single entity and give it a name.

By sharing with you my own expert insights, the three-model system, I have demonstrated how this works for my business. To review:

1. First, I shared my problem model, The Repumeter™. You need a problem model that brings your prospects' or audiences' awareness to a problem they never knew they had.

2. Then I shared my cost model which demonstrated how your current position on your own Repumeter™ was affecting your business in terms of influence, impact and income. You need to be able to make your audiences and prospects present to the cost of having the problem you just revealed.

3. I selected three primary currencies: influence, impact and income. I selected these because they are the primary currencies of my audience: speakers, coaches, authors, consultants, and sales professionals. You need to know what the most relevant currencies are to your clients.

4. Then I shared the cause model which demonstrated what most prospects do that keep them in the wrong spot on the Repumeter™; they focus on their solution. You need to know what your prospects are doing wrong or not doing at all that is keeping them stuck in the wrong spot on your problem model.

5. Then I introduced the concept of expert insights as my solution. This solution positions me as the only logical choice because I am the only one who provides it under this name. Your solution will be called something else. It should position you as the only logical choice because you are the only one who provides it under whatever name you give it.

If you can do all of this for your audiences and prospects, you'll have taken an enormous step toward appearing to be profoundly different no matter what your profession is.

I have several one-on-one clients with whom I work on this material. It sometimes takes months to find the expert insights. You must challenge and question it, twist and turn it in myriad ways. It is not a quick fix and it takes time and effort. When you are ready to present your system to the world, it should be almost unquestionable, almost unchallengeable. You need to be able to use examples to support your claims. You should be able to draw it on a napkin or show it on a big screen. Remember, it should work for every size audience!

A Testimonial

To help put all of this into context for you, here's a short note from a friend and client who has gone through the entire deep thought strategy process with me:

As a friend, admirer, colleague and student of Steve's, here's my 2 cents worth regarding this process of formalizing your expert insights, developing your model(s), and positioning yourself in a crowded marketplace.

This is not EASY.

Having worked at conferences and conventions where Steve was also presenting, I thought I understood the process. We had numerous discussions about his program, his process, and this book. It wasn't until I actually went through the process with Steve that it all clicked for me at the level necessary for me to truly "get it," internalize it and integrate it into my own business.

Steve is adept at asking questions that allowed me to get to my own answers, my own expert insights, my own model. He asked simple but challenging questions, allowed me to explore potential answers and guided me, without making me feel pushed or frustrated, to the answers I needed to discover to complete the process. That's his gift as well as his skill and expertise.

The timeframe for going through the process is different for everyone Steve works with and there are a variety of delivery mechanisms that work. Face-to-face, one-on-one is what worked for me.

At the outset I said, "I'm not sure I even need expert insights!"

I had no expectations of the outcome except I knew I needed to understand the process at a more organic and authentic level.

I knew my strengths in terms of expertise and experience. I knew why I wanted my clients to hire me (besides revenue generation to pay my mortgage) and what results I wanted them to achieve.

We actually worked backwards, as Stephen Covey said by "beginning with the end in mind."

Starting with the desired result, I was able to tap into my own expert insights (through Steve's questioning process and our subsequent discussions) based on my experience and expertise focusing on the development of a sliding scale model for levels of influence. Once all that came together, a program title emerged which is unique and will provide my clients with a problem they didn't know they had and the urgency to address it because the cost of ignoring it is too important not to fix. (Surprise: I apparently did need a model and I'm thrilled!)

*In a very short period of time, all the pieces I thought I understood prior to my time with Steve came together for me, enhancing not only my own knowledge, but giving me a tool that I can use one-on-one or from the stage, facing a large audience. **Being able to address those two opportunities with the same model, the same expert insights and achieve the same results is priceless.***

After having gone through the deep thought strategy and finding my own expert insights, I have a whole new direction for the next chapter of my speaking career. Just a few months after I completed the work with Steve, I am already being sought after to appear on international stages for my new and innovative content around legacy.

CONCLUSION

Is thinking big the wrong thing to do? Of course not! It simply needs to be part of a strategy, not the strategy itself.

The deep thought strategy process will provide you with something that gives you fuel when launching a bigger campaign or pursuing a bigger goal, your expert insights.

Before thinking bigger, think deeper. Find your expert insights and craft them well. Learn to present them tactically and then do so. Present your expert insights often and everywhere. Guide the conversation so your circles associate your name with the results you provide, the experience you provide and most importantly, your expert insights.

Migrate your circle of connection over to your circle of influence and watch your Repumeter™ position move swiftly towards the state of THE One where you become the only logical choice.

It's at this point when you are ready to think and execute bigger.

Always remember, you don't actually have to be different from anyone else who does what you do, you only have to appear to be different. Your expert insights are what make you appear to be different.

Change the language you use, help people repeat your message through your expert insights and play a bigger game.

Valuable lessons from my time with Brian the tennis instructor.

ABOUT THE AUTHOR

Steve Lowell has been speaking and performing on the live stage since the age of 6; that's over 50 years ago.

From Ottawa, Canada, Steve is an award-winning, global speaker and for over 30 years he has been training and mentoring executives, thought-leaders and professional speakers around the world to deliver high-impact keynote speeches, drive revenue from the platform and build wealth through speaking.

He's the past national President of the Canadian Association of Professional Speakers (CAPS) and the 2021 President of the Global Speakers Federation (GSF)

He is one of fewer than 12% of the world's professional speakers to hold the Certified Speaking Professional (CSP) designation; the highest designation in professional speaking. He shares the stage with such greats as Jack Canfield (*Chicken Soup for the Soul* Series), Kevin Harrington (*Shark Tank* and "As Seen on TV"), Grant Cardone (*The 10X Rule*) and Brian Tracy (Author of over 70 books).

Together with his wife Jayne, he travels the world speaking, training and mentoring those who have a message to monetize through the spoken word.

Want to Learn More?

Whenever you're ready... here are three ways we can help you design your 'Expert Insights" through your own "Deep Thought Strategy" to drive business without the pitch.

1. **Register for our e-learning course and be a part of our global Facebook community**
Our entry-level online training program is a superb start if you are wanting to get started on your own "Deep Thought Strategy". Begin by discovering your own "Expert Insights" at www.BigMoneyMessage.com

2. **Join one of our Implementation Programs and be a Case Study**
We offer small case study groups (maximum 6 participants) who learn how to craft and implement their "Expert Insights" and then become a case study to demonstrate the power of the 'Expert Insights" concepts. This is by application only. To apply, send an email to hello@thelowells.global with the subject "Case Study Group"

3. **Work with Us Privately**
If you'd like to work directly or privately with us to implement your "Deep Thought Strategy", just send us a message at hello@thelowells.global and with the word "Private"... tell us a little about your business and what you'd like to work on together, and we'll get you all the details!

Giving a Voice to Creativity!

Your donation will give a voice to the creativity
that lies within the hearts of physically,
spiritually and mentally challenged children.

By helping us publish their books,
musical creations and works of art you will
make a difference in a child's life;
a child who would not otherwise be heard.

Donate now by going to
HeartstobeHeard.com

The children thank you!!